TALKING ABOUT
FREEDOM

TALKING ABOUT FREEDOM

CELEBRATING EMANCIPATION DAY IN CANADA

Natasha L. Henry

DUNDURN
NATURAL HERITAGE
TORONTO

Editor: Matt Baker
Design: Jesse Hooper
Printer: Marquis

Library and Archives Canada Cataloguing in Publication

Henry, Natasha L.
    Talking about freedom : celebrating Emancipation Day in Canada / by Natasha L. Henry.

Issued also in electronic formats.
ISBN 978-1-4597-0048-2

    1. Emancipation Day (Canada)--Juvenile literature.   2. Slaves--Emancipation--Canada--Juvenile literature.   3. Black Canadians--History--Juvenile literature.   4. Africans--Canada--History--Juvenile literature.   I. Title.

FC106.B6H463 2012   j394.263   C2011-903856-0

1   2   3   4   5   16   15   14   13   12

We acknowledge the support of the **Canada Council for the Arts** and the **Ontario Arts Council** for our publishing program. We also acknowledge the financial support of the **Government of Canada** through the **Canada Book Fund** and **Livres Canada Books**, and the **Government of Ontario** through the **Ontario Book Publishing Tax Credit** and the **Ontario Media Development Corporation**.

Care has been taken to trace the ownership of copyright material used in this book. The author and the publisher welcome any information enabling them to rectify any references or credits in subsequent editions.

J. Kirk Howard, President

Printed and bound in Canada.
www.dundurn.com

Dundurn	Gazelle Book Services Limited	Dundurn
3 Church Street, Suite 500	White Cross Mills	2250 Military Road
Toronto, Ontario, Canada	High Town, Lancaster, England	Tonawanda, NY
M5E 1M2	LA1 4XS	U.S.A. 14150

This book is dedicated to my beautiful, brilliant daughter, Jamaya.

CONTENTS

ACKNOWLEDGEMENTS

My family has been the core of my strength and motivation during the course of writing this book. I would like to express my heartfelt appreciation to my partner Fitzroy and my daughter Jamaya for being understanding when I was out researching or on the computer writing for endless hours; to Mommy, Nicole, and Simone for taking good care of Jamaya; my brothers Gary and Desroy for their encouragement; and my extended family in Canada and the United States for their support.

I wish to express my sincere thanks to the following people and institutions, who helped to make the completion of this book an easier task: Rawle Thompson; Denise Stern; Hilary Dawson, genealogist and historical researcher; Spencer Alexander and the Buxton Museum; Cherylyn Hansler; Brian Gilchrist, Region of Peel Archives; Irene Moore Davis, Essex County Black Historical Research Society; Blair Newby, Chatham-Kent Black Historical Society; Wilberforce University Archives; the *Hamilton Spectator*; Margaret Houghton, Hamilton Public Library's special collections; the Marsh Historical Collection Society; Karolyn Smardz Frost and Henry Bishop, the Black Cultural Centre for Nova Scotia; and the Norval Johnson Heritage Library and Nathaniel Dett Chapel.

I am honoured to have received guidance from elders Wilma Morrison and Gwen Robinson, who understand the importance of passing on the rich history of African Canadians. I am also very grateful to Beth Allen, Blaine Courtney, Adrienne Shadd, Dennis Scott, and Nerene Virgin for sharing their personal experiences and family history with me. Several young people have also provided their insight, which has proven to be invaluable — thank you Raulandre, Breanna, and Bria.

Barry Penhale and Jane Gibson of Natural Heritage Books have provided tremendous guidance and support throughout the course of this project, and I thank them for that. I am also thankful to Dundurn for providing the platform to share the history of this significant Canadian cultural tradition.

I would like to acknowledge the financial support of the Ontario Arts Council through the Writer's Reserve program in the completion of this project.

INTRODUCTION

"When I get older, I will be stronger,
they'll call me freedom, just like a waving flag."
— "Waving Flag," K'Naan, *Troubadour*, 2009

Young Canadians today embrace freedom of expression, and this permits talented, vocal individuals to reach others through various genres of writing, art, and music. It is no coincidence that songs, books, and paintings — media that everyone can relate to — are used to communicate the need for freedom and to preserve the history of the past struggles.

Why has the song "Waving Flag" resonated with people around the world? People can relate to K'Naan's experience. Some have gone through similar experiences of escaping war, surviving, and going on to achieve personal success. In a general sense, the song expresses the universal story of overcoming insurmountable obstacles in one's life, the hope of freedom, and the fulfilment of one's aspirations. It was covered by a group of Canadian music artists, Young Artists for Haiti, in relief efforts for Haiti after the catastrophic January 2010 earthquake. "Waving

Flag" was also selected as the anthem for the 2010 International Federation of Association Football (FIFA) World Cup Trophy Tour, and it was recorded in numerous versions with singers from different countries.

K'Naan, born Keinan Abdi Warsame in Mogadishu, Somalia, in 1978, fled with his family to Canada to escape the Somali Civil War, which began in 1991. K'Naan's hit song, and his music as a whole, is influenced by his experiences growing up in Somalia. Freedom, victory over evil, refuge, and opportunity in Canada is not just K'Naan's story. It is the life journey of many people, past and present, world-wide, who can relate to experiencing war, social injustice, and forms of enslavement. The chorus of the song — "When I get older / I will be stronger / They'll call me freedom / Just like a waving flag" — is a courageous declaration that liberty and freedom can never ultimately be denied to those who seek it.

The comparison of freedom to a waving flag is a vivid metaphor: a flag soars in the wind, unrestricted. A flag represents the promise of freedom, refuge, and opportunity, the ideals of a country, of loyalty, patriotism, national pride, as well as security and the protection of one's rights and civil liberties. All of these concepts have been celebrated the world over by individuals fortunate enough to live in countries at a time when they expressed such sentiments.

In Canada, 1834, then known as Upper and Lower Canada, one such free-dom festival began when the enslavement of people of African descent was abol-ished. People came together to celebrate freedom and the ideals that Canada now symbolizes, and this led to a longstanding African-Canadian cultural tradition: Emancipation Day. For this annual celebration, Blacks from Canada and the United States, people of European background, and members of First Nations groups assembled in many towns across Ontario and Quebec, the Maritime prov-inces of Nova Scotia and New Brunswick, and in British Columbia. As of 2011, Emancipation Day has been commemorated in Canada on August 1 for 177 years.

Freedom has been the constant theme of Emancipation Day, but even though enslaved Blacks were freed, in the following decades African Canadians had to fight for the full rights and privileges they were entitled to as citizens, because of the racial discrimination they faced in their daily lives.

And so, true freedom remained in the distance and Blacks in Canada persistently pursued it. Thus, the celebration of freedom on the August First was also a call for people to address inequality. Emancipation Day evolved over time, developing its own unique traditional elements and cultural rituals. It grew to include numerous activities, events, and incorporated political activism, raising racial consciousness, and fostering community development with the purpose of breaking down racial barriers and moving toward a life of equality.

CHAPTER ONE

OH, FREEDOM!

Freedom, freedom.
Wanna thank you, freedom.
There's nothing in the world like freedom.
— "FREEDOM (INTRO)," ANGIE STONE, *BLACK DIAMOND*, 1999

The idea of freedom has both moral and legal aspects. All human beings have natural rights, and these rights are considered to be universal in progressive societies. Some examples of inherent rights include the rights to life, freedom, and citizenship, including the rights to vote, live, and work in a particular place. Then there are legal rights, which are granted and enforced by a government as specified by the laws it passes. A couple of examples include the right to be treated fairly when arrested or detained, and the right to a safe workplace.

To be free means to have the ability to do what you would like within legal limits, to enjoy political and civil rights, to go where you want, to meet with who you want, and to have some measure of control over your life. A free person can also exercise the right to an education, the right to vote, the right to live where one chooses, and the right to practise his or her religion of choice.

When African men and women were kidnapped from Africa, beginning in 1441, first by the Portuguese and then France and Britain, they were denied their natural and legal rights by the kidnappers, merchants, and masters that enslaved them. Enslaved Africans were deemed to be movable property, meaning they were not considered to be human, but instead as commodities like furniture, cows, horses, and tools. Africans were bought, sold, bartered, given as gifts, and bequeathed in wills. Further, as property they had very few, if any, legal rights in the new lands they were forcibly taken to. Of course, they resisted their captivity as best they could, whether during the raids on their villages in Africa, in the holding pens at the ports of West Africa, on slave ships at sea, or in the New World.

Enslaved peoples of African descent challenged their status as slaves through various levels of resistance, from breaking work tools to more dangerous acts, like running away or organizing armed rebellions. The Haitian Revolution, which lasted from 1791 to 1804, was a successful major slave revolt. It resulted in the abolition of slavery on that island and independence from French rule, making The Republic of Haiti the first Black republic in the Western hemisphere.

Other slave rebellions include the 1570 revolt led by Gabon native Gaspar Yanga in Mexico. The enslaved Africans escaped and built a small *Maroon* community that survived for almost thirty years. Maroons were Africans taken to the Caribbean who resisted slavery by running away. They established settlements in the mountains of various islands and protected themselves from recapture by fighting either British, Portuguese, or Spanish colonists. The First Maroon War with the British lasted from 1720 to 1739, and was led by Cudjoe, his sister Nanny, and an Asante woman, as well as other brave women and men. The conflict continued to the end of the eighteenth century. Approximately six hundred Maroons agreed to relocate to Nova Scotia as one of the terms of peace after the Second Maroon War (1795–1796). Today, the only surviving Maroon community is in

Accompong, St. Elizabeth, in western Jamaica. They continue to live separately from the wider Jamaican society and are still governed symbolically by the peace treaty signed with the British in 1739, which officially ended in 1962.

There were also many slave uprisings in the United States, including the Stono Rebellion in South Carolina, in September 1739, where about one hundred enslaved African Americans walked down the road, carrying a banner that read, LIBERTY!, and shouted the word as they marched along. The group stole guns, and by the end of that morning, many White slave owners and their families had lost their lives, totalling twenty-five deaths. They were confronted by a large group of armed White men, who killed one-third of the rebels. Within the next month, most of the other fugitives were found and executed.

The largest American slave rebellion was the January 1811 German Coast Uprising in the Territory of Orleans. A band of over one hundred enslaved men and women marched towards New Orleans, with more men joining as they walked. The group grew to almost five hundred. Armed with hand tools, they burned down five plantation homes, as well as sugarhouses and several acres of crops, on their way to New Orleans. A militia of White men formed to suppress the rebels, and by the end of the two-day insurrection, two Whites and almost one hundred Blacks were killed. Forty-four more escapees were tried and executed over the next two weeks. These revolts give an indication of just how far Blacks worldwide were willing to go to be free, even giving their lives for the cause.

At the beginning of the transatlantic slave trade, males who were strong labourers made up more than half of the human cargo. Later, more females were enslaved because they could reproduce and increase the labour force. Approximately twenty million Africans, most of them young men and women, were permanently removed from their homes and taken across the Atlantic Ocean — a horrendous trip called the Middle Passage. This voyage, from the west coast of Africa to the New World, took between two to three long months. The captives were chained up below deck and occasionally given time for stretching and exercise, but overall the conditions were wretched. During the over three hundred years that the Middle Passage was in operation, between five to eight million enslaved Africans died because of malnutrition, poor sanitation, and the spread of disease aboard the overcrowded slave ships.

Africans were enslaved in European colonies throughout the Atlantic World, including Canada, where the earliest recorded African slave was Olivier LeJeune. He came from the African island of Madagascar, located in the Indian Ocean off the southeastern coast of the African continent. In 1628 the six-year-old LeJeune was sold by an English merchant to a government official in New France, now Quebec. While this is certainly an early instance, the practice of slavery in Canada first began with the enslavement of Aboriginals by the French. The French also enslaved some Africans in Quebec and the Maritime provinces. However, when the British gained control of both Upper and Lower Canada in 1763, after the Seven Years' War, the number of enslaved Africans increased.

Slaves were used as free labour for the development of the colonies. Their jobs included cutting trees to clear the land, building homes and roads, farming, and working in European homes as domestic servants. Many slaves worked in skilled occupations as blacksmiths, wainwrights, coopers, and wheelwrights.

How slaves were treated depended on the owner. Some of the harsher treatments endured by Canadian slaves included whippings, being jailed for petty offenses, and being sentenced to death by hanging. Loyalist Matthew Elliot, who settled on his land grant in Fort Malden (now Amherstburg), brought over sixty slaves with him after the American Revolutionary War. In the front of his estate, he had an iron whipping-post on a tree, where his slaves were tied and beaten as punishment — remember, slaves in Canada were considered property, a fact so taken for granted that they were even sold privately through local newspapers. Some, however, received fairer treatment. Their owners allowed to them to learn how to read and write. Some slaves were manumitted, or released from slavery, when their owner died, and some were compensated with money, land, or heirlooms for their years of service.

The enslaved Africans in the Atlantic world were determined to be free, and by the early nineteenth century they were receiving a lot of support from people known as abolitionists, who wanted to end of the barbaric system of slavery. There was growing pressure from these abolitionist groups, both Black and White, in Europe, North America, and the Caribbean to demand an end to slavery. In order for the trade and enslavement of Africans to end, it first had to be made illegal. The first anti-slavery law in the British colonies was the 1793 Act to Limit Slavery, which was passed in Upper Canada, now called Ontario. This law was introduced by Lieutenant-Governor John Graves Simcoe, himself an abolitionist. But this law did not free any slaves, because of strong opposition from several government officials who owned slaves. Instead, the Act to Limit Slavery would gradually abolish the practice over a twenty-five year period.

For sale, for three years, from the 29th of this present month of July,

A Negro Wench,

Named Chloe, 23 years old, understands washing, cooking, &c. Any gentleman wishing to purchase, or employ her by the year or month, is requested to apply to   ROBERT FRANKLIN,
at the receiver general's,
Newark, July 25, 1795.   34tf.

An advertisement for a young Black enslaved woman for sale in Newark in the Niagara area. Newark was the capital of Upper Canada (Ontario) until 1797, when Simcoe moved his administrative centre to York (Toronto).

From the *Upper Canada Gazette*, August 19, 1795.

Abolitionists were finally successful, when, in August of 1833, the British Parliament enacted the Slavery Abolition Act, which freed over 800,000 enslaved Africans. This act owed its existence to the persistence of African people in working toward their freedom — efforts that eventually gained support from White British abolitionists. The act declared that, under the British flag, Blacks were human beings under the law and that one person did not have the right to own another person. It stated, "Whereas divers Persons are holden in Slavery, within divers of His Majesty's Colonies, and it is just and expedient that all such Persons should be manumitted and set free ..."[1] The enslavement of Africans in other regions continued, with slavery being abolished in Danish and French colonies in 1848, including the Virgin Islands, Martinique, and Guadeloupe; Dutch colonies such as Suriname and Saint Maarten in 1863; and the United States of America in 1865. The latest abolitions in the Atlantic World took place in Cuba in 1886 and Brazil in 1888.

WORDPLAY

An *indentured servant* was someone who agreed to contract their labour for a set time to an employer, usually between three to seven years. In exchange for their labour, indentured servants received shelter, food, and clothing. The idea behind the introduction of indentured servitude was to allow former slave owners to continue to have access to a cheap pool of labour.

August 1, 1834, was a significant day throughout the English-speaking Caribbean. Soon-to-be freed slaves attended churches the night before and waited eagerly for the dawning of the new day, when they could celebrate their first day of freedom. Services that included sermons and singing were held. Then thousands took to the streets, joining with fellow freepersons in festivities such as parading, dancing, listening to music, singing, watching plays, and enjoying a variety of food.

However, on islands such as Jamaica and Barbados, and in Guyana and South Africa, the formerly enslaved were not fully free, and instead became indentured servants to their former owners. They would have to wait until August 1, 1838, to be completely free. Since then, on every August First, the liberation of enslaved Africans and the idea of freedom has been celebrated in the West Indies, parts of the United States, and Canada. A new tradition was born.

CHAPTER TWO

FREE AT LAST!

Turn me loose — it's now or never.
Feel like I could run forever.
A new day's come, a new moon's risin',
I take my chances on the blue horizon.
A leap of faith, a shot of spirit,
Freedom's callin', I can hear it.
— "It Ain't Over Yet," Bryan Adams, *Racing Stripes* Soundtrack, 2004

The annual African-Canadian tradition of Emancipation Day was born on August 1, 1834, when *An Act for the Abolition of Slavery throughout the British Colonies; for promoting the Industry of the manumitted slaves; and for compensating the Persons hitherto entitled to the Service of such Slaves* came into effect.[1] Called the Slavery Abolition Act for short, it liberated over 800,000 enslaved Africans from most British colonies, such as Antigua, Bermuda, and Trinidad, but it also included a small number in Canada. Britain did not want planters to remove their slaves and plantations to other territories that still practised slavery, as it would affect

Britain's economy, so they were offered a payout by the British government. Slave owners shared twenty-million English pounds in compensation for this loss of slaves, while ex-slaves did not receive any compensation.

Following abolition an apprenticeship system was immediately implemented in Jamaica, Guyana, Barbados, and South Africa. The argument behind the apprenticeship program was that it would assist former slave owners in transitioning into a new way of operating their businesses and help the formerly enslaved to prepare for full freedom. Under the program, people who were enslaved now became apprentices, meaning that their labour still belonged to someone else for free, but now only for a specific period of time, in this case six years. Of course, this new arrangement was also designed with the intention of providing plantation owners with continued free labour. Not surprisingly, this program was unpopular with the workers, and because of many difficulties, it ended early on August 1, 1838, granting all former slaves in the British colonies complete and full freedom. The day that slaves received their freedom was a joyous occasion, and they celebrated by thanking and praising God at church for releasing them from bondage. They marched and danced through streets and plantations, enjoyed feasts, and generally shared their joy with one another.

Ever since that day, freed men and women, abolitionists, and sympathizers have come together on August First in British territories as well as Canada and parts of the Northern United States to celebrate West Indian Emancipation Day. Emancipation Day observances later incorporated the end of American slavery when it was abolished in 1865. Another day, often called "Lincoln Day," was added to the celebration to mark this historic moment. "The first day was the celebration of the West Indies and the second day the Lincoln."[2]

Emancipation Day was one of the most anticipated days of the year for Black Canadians. The abolition of the enslavement of Africans in British colonies was commemorated in villages, towns, and large centres in Canada with street processions, speeches, banquets, balls, concerts, and church services. August First has been commemorated in places across Canada, with the majority of celebra-tions taking occurring in Ontario:

Montreal, Quebec	St. Catharines
Halifax, Nova Scotia	Niagara Falls
Saint John, New Brunswick	Brantford
Victoria, British Columbia	Owen Sound
Chatham	Queen's Bush
Dawn	Collingwood
Dresden	Oro
London	Amherstburg
Norwich	Sandwich
Hamilton	Windsor
Oakville	Kitchener
Toronto	

This historic occasion led to the creation of an African-Canadian tradition that included many aspects of Black life — religious, educational, economic, political, and social. August First, once also called West India Day, was celebrated every year for several reasons. African Canadians wanted to show appreciation to Britain for granting them freedom and the opportunity to build a new life. The recognition of Emancipation Day also served to put the southern United States on notice, warning them of the sure end of American slavery through constant campaigning. The occasion was also intended to show unity with Blacks in the English-speaking Caribbean, to express a group identity as people who originated from Africa, and to express their shared qualities and values as members of the human race. Soon after August First, 1834, it also became a chance to air their grievances about racial discrimination. The festivities attracted scores of people from across each province — from places like Ottawa, Montreal, and Halifax — and many guests also attended from all corners of the United States.

Freedom from slavery became a reality after four centuries of enslavement and resistance. The seeds of promise, hope, and justice were planted.

CHAPTER THREE

THE ORGANIZATION OF EMANCIPATION DAY FESTIVITIES

I have a dream, I gotta find my way.
My dream is to be free.
— "I Have a Dream," Common, featuring Will.I.Am,
Freedom Writers Soundtrack, 2006

Emancipation Day celebrations in Canada attracted hundreds and thousands of people each year, requiring extensive preparations to ensure a smooth-running event. Planning began months in advance, and planning committees were formed to organize the Emancipation Day programme. These committee groups consisted of men and women of different social, educational, and economic backgrounds, including teachers, church ministers, lawyers, small business owners, and blue collar workers: "A committee of the coloured population had been long formed to carry their plans into execution and to invite delegates from various settlements to join their procession, and partake of the bountiful fare which they had provided."[1] Early Emancipation Day committee members included *Voice of the Fugitive* founder Henry Bibb and Reverend Josiah Henson, co-founder of the Dawn Settlement for fugitive slaves.

Emancipation Day commemorative events were major celebrations, usually running from one to four days in length, and they drew a huge number of people from all facets of society. This was an exciting period for Black Canadians as friends and family came together to express their solidarity.

August First events were organized by African-Canadian cultural and social institutions. Churches, including the British Methodist Episcopal (BME), African Methodist Episcopal (AME), Baptist, Anglican, and Presbyterian churches, sponsored commemorations. Temperance societies — groups that spoke out against the excessive drinking of alcohol, like the Hawkesville and Windsor temperance societies — arranged observances as well. Another group, the Toronto Abolition Society (also known as the British-American Anti-Slavery Society), formed in 1833, was an anti-slavery organization established by Black Torontonians, and they planned Emancipation Day celebrations in Toronto in the 1830s and 1840s.

In Windsor the British American Association of Colored Brothers (BAACB) was responsible for the massive celebrations in that city from 1931 to 1967. Aside from making Emancipation Day "the greatest freedom show on earth," another objective of the BAACB was to challenge discrimination in all its forms. Another group, the London-based Canadian League for the Advancement of Coloured People (CLACP), was created by James F. Jenkins, owner of the London Black newspaper the *Dawn of Tomorrow*, and a man named J. W. Montgomery, of Toronto. The organization focused on fighting racial discrimination and anti-Black sentiment in various facets of society. They also worked to foster unity between Black cultural institutions in Canada. During the 1930s, CLACP conducted annual excursions to Springbank Park in London to celebrate Emancipation Day.

In Jamaica, on August 1, 1914, Jamaican Marcus Mosiah Garvey founded the Universal Negro Improvement Association (UNIA), an international organization for people of African descent. The Toronto chapter sponsored the "Big Picnic" in St. Catharines from the 1920s to the1950s, and the chapter in Montreal also organized a yearly Emancipation Day picnic in the 1920s and 1930s. The

Toronto Emancipation Committee, under the leadership of Donald Moore, hosted Emancipation Day commemorations in the 1950s and 1960s.

✳ ✳ ✳

Robert Dunn (front, centre), Grand Master, with fellow members of the Freeman Lodge, the Windsor chapter of the Grand United Order of Oddfellows, at Wigle Park in Windsor, Ontario, in 1922.

Courtesy of the E. Andrea Shreve Moore Collection, Essex County Black Historical Research Society.

Masonic lodges are societies of freemasons, fraternal organizations that provide an opportunity for men to enjoy the company of friends, improve themselves, and help others through charity. Some African-Canadian lodges involved in the planning of Emancipation Day festivities include the Damascus Commandery #4 and the Lincoln Lodge #8, both in Amherstburg; the Peter Ogden Lodge No. 812, in Toronto; and the Mount Brydges Lodge No. 1865 of Hamilton. Recently, Black heritage sites like the North American Black Historical Museum, Griffin House at the Fieldcote Memorial Park and Museum, and Uncle Tom's Cabin Historic Site have undertaken the task of reviving Emancipation Day celebrations.

By providing much-needed support systems, these associations and many others like them played a vital role in the lives of African Canadians. Today, African-Canadian heritage sites focus on preserving the memory of Blacks' contributions to Canada, and celebrating this significant milestone in the history of people of African ancestry is a natural part of their efforts to uplift the spirit of the community and educate the masses.

The scheduling of the location, date, and time of celebrations had to be done months in advance, and sometimes a particular theme was selected for that year. In order to use streets for parades or public buildings for certain activities, organizers had to apply for permits from city governments. To appeal to as many people as possible, a variety of entertainers, bands, and speakers were hired. Then, venues like parks for picnics, halls for parties, and dances for after the day programmes came to an end had to be booked.

Imagine having to ensure that there was enough food to feed 10,000 people in one day! The organizing committees coordinated the preparation of literally tons of food for huge groups of festival goers. They also had to make plans for the transportation of both

PLANNING FOR SUCCESS

The committee of management — also called the planning committee, the committee of arrangements, or the organizing committee — was very important for the success of the numerous events. What community festival have you attended recently? The CHIN Picnic at the Exhibition Grounds in Toronto? The Beaches International Jazz Festival in Toronto? What kinds of games, activities, and performers were there? Just like the local festivals we go to today, there was a lot to do to prepare for the arrival of large crowds and to make the event a memorable occasion for visitors.

local guests and out-of-town tourists. Today, celebrants can use public transit, drive a car, or if they are coming from the United States, can take an airplane. Contemporary events also offer free shuttle service. However, in the nineteenth-century, planning committees organized ticket deals with railway, ferry, and coach companies such as the Grand Truck Railway and the Dalhousie Navigation Company for people without their own means of travel.

Large-scale festivals sometimes arranged accommodations with hotels and inns for visitors staying overnight, but it was common at one time for local homes to offer lodging for guests. Well into the 1960s, Emancipation Day planners would liaison with restaurants and hotels — those who would accept Black patrons — in order to ensure proper accommodations.[2]

Another important aspect of planning festivals was providing a wide range of appealing activities for participants of all ages and tastes. It was customary to extend invitations to special guests, such as politicians, celebrities, community leaders, and other dignitaries from near and abroad — their presence added more to the occasion.

While ticket sales were the biggest way organizers made money to cover the costs of running the festival, attendees were also able to pay admission at the door. In 1962 an advance ticket to Windsor's Emancipation Day celebration at Jackson Park cost $1.00, and the gate admission was $1.50!

The president or chairman, the head of the planning committee, made sure the committees worked as a team and completed their assigned tasks. Past presidents include Reverend D. J. Hulbert of the First Baptist Church, in Amherstburg in 1928; Walter Perry of the British America Association of Colored Brothers (BAACB), in Windsor from 1931 to 1967; and Dennis Scott of the Emancipation Festival in Owen Sound, from 2000 to 2010. Scott describes "the pride in following

Railway companies such as the Great Western Railway and the Canadian Pacific Railway offered special rates to travellers attending Emancipation day celebrations.

The Windsor Evening Record, July 31, 1894.

in the footsteps of community leaders" as immeasurable. The vice-president or vice-chairman assisted the president and filled in for the president during their absence.

SPOTLIGHT ON ...

In 2011 Blaine Courtney became the chair of the Owen Sound Emancipation Day Festival Board. He was born and raised in Owen Sound. His family have been in Canada for four generations, and his great-grandfather, a runaway slave from the Courtney plantation in the Carolinas, made his way to freedom by means of the Underground Railroad.

SPOTLIGHT ON ...

Walter Perry, "Mr. Emancipation," was born in Chatham in 1899. He was the great-grandson of fugitive slaves. Walter grew up in Windsor.

Walter Perry was affectionately called "Mr. Emancipation."

Courtesy of the E. Andrea Shreve Moore Collection, Essex County Black Historical Research Society.

The secretary of the committee recorded the minutes (a record of discussions and decisions of meetings) and handled all correspondence with potential guests, involved companies, and city departments. James B. Hollinsworth was the secretary for the 1857 Dresden committee, Phillip Smith was the secretary for the 1892 Toronto committee, and Winifred Shreve was secretary of the BAACB's Emancipation Day Committee through the 1950s and 1960s.

The secretary had to be able to read and write, which was uncommon in the years before the abolition of American slavery — in many southern states, it was against the law to teach slaves to read and write. Some Whites who supported slavery believed that this would prevent Blacks from learning about race equality and the arguments against slavery. Furthermore, slave owners thought an education was not necessary for a slave to work in the fields or in the slave master's

Winifred Shreve (second from left) was active in numerous areas of Windsor's Black community. Her efforts of preserving African-Canadian history have continued on through her daughter, E. Andrea Shreve Moore, and grand-daughter, Irene Moore Davis, president of the Essex County Black Historical Research Society.

Courtesy of the E. Andrea Shreve Moore Collection, Essex County Black Historical Research Society.

house. Still, some slaves learned to read, write, and do math in secret; they were taught by other slaves, free Blacks, or liberal-minded Whites. Free Blacks living in northern states were able to go to school and learn.

Financial matters related to organizing Emancipation Day could be very demanding. The treasurer kept track of all the money brought in. At times, donations were collected for specific causes connected to the Black community, such as social programs for young people. As the celebrations grew in size, new financial concerns had to be addressed, like providing parking spaces for visitors or compensating speakers, marching bands, and other performers for their time and travel. Sometimes, fees were charged for using city-run parks: festivals hosted on city property had to be insured in case of accidents or damage, and paid duty police officers had to be hired to patrol public locations. Another way to obtain funding was to solicit local businesses to purchase advertisement spots in programme booklets, including the ones published inside *Progress* magazine in Windsor.

As the treasurer in the 1960s, Alice Anna Allen prepared financial reports at the end of the yearly celebrations. She noted, "It is expected that the receipts will well meet the disbursements when all collections are in."[3] In other words, organizers were expected to collect enough money to pay for the expenses.

Subcommittees were formed to cover various aspects of the organization of Emancipation Day. For example, the program subcommittee assisted planning the program of activities. Fundraising Committees were created to raise money that would help the development of the Black community throughout the year. In 1851 money was raised for building the Sandwich First Baptist Church. In 1869 a club from Detroit proposed that a concert be held in Chatham on August First, with the proceeds to go to the Nazrey Institute, a school organized by Reverends Willis Nazrey, Richard Randolph Disney, and Walter Hawkins that same year. The school educated over sixty students and had six teachers.[4] Money was also raised for scholarships to assist students who wished to attend high school or specialized programs — before the late nineteenth century, secondary education was not part of the public school system and was typically paid for by parents. Higher levels of education were important for Blacks, both for individual success and the progress of the Black community as a whole.

In 1891 in St. Catharines, fundraising proceeds went to aid the BME church Salem Chapel. The profits of the evening programme in Chatham in 1871 went to the Widow and Orphan's Fund of the St. John's Lodge No. 9 in Chatham. In 1935 the Emancipation Day picnic was a fundraiser for the church and school building in Wallenstein in the Queen's Bush area, which was located southwest of Lake Huron and included parts of present-day Wellington County and Waterloo County, as well as Dufferin, Grey, and Bruce Counties. These funds were also used to help with the daily operations of the various institutions that were of great benefit to community members. In those days, there were no government grants like there are today to support running community programs. Organizations and individuals had to be creative in coming up with ways to raise money to maintain their survival.

Womens' committees were regularly formed to unite African-Canadian women to address their concerns and needs. They were also an excellent platform to showcase the work Black women were doing in the community. In Sandwich in 1851, Mary Bibb — wife of newspaper founder and abolitionist Henry Bibb — and other women, including Jane Hawkins, Sophia East, Winnie Hoover, Lucretia Brown, Eliza Brent, as well as the wives of Henry Turner and Robert Ward, prepared dinner and refreshments for sale in support of the building fund for the Sandwich First Baptist Church.

In particular, there was strong female involvement in the planning of Emancipation Day celebration in Windsor in 1954. The Hour-A-Day Study Club and the BAACB invited African-American civil rights activist Mary McLeod Bethune and former first lady Eleanor Roosevelt as guest speakers. Both women were very accomplished and active in improving the social conditions of people around the world. Mary McLeod Bethune was the founder and president of Bethune-Cookman College in Daytona Beach, Florida. She was also one of the advisors to President Franklin Delano Roosevelt on the "Black Cabinet." This group was formed to advise the president's administration on the concerns of African Americans. For her part, Eleanor Roosevelt travelled around the world advocating for human rights and encouraging the public to become active in making the world a better place.

This was the first time in the history of the commemoration of Emancipation Day that women were part of the lineup of key speakers. In 1958 International Women's Day was held as part of the Emancipation Day celebration in Windsor, organized by the female members of the planning committee who were also members of the Hour-A-Day Study Club. The all-women's program included guest speaker Irene Gaines of Chicago, president of the International Association of Colored Women's Clubs of America. Also involved were the Michigan Women's Choral Ensemble and Windsor soprano-singer Hazel Solomon. African-Canadian women have always played key roles in organizing the annual freedom festival. Their involvement was important to the success of August First.

Another Emancipation Day standing committee was the games committee. Selected committee members organized all of the athletic and sporting activities held at public parks. They selected a range of traditional picnic games like sack and three-legged races, along with other competitive and fun games that would appeal to participants young and old.

On the day of the event, the president of the management committee or an elected chairman of the day called the assembly to order, greeted the audience, proclaimed the meeting legally assembled, opened the exercises for the day, introduced the speakers, reminded people to conduct themselves with respect, and stated the reason for the gathering. The African-Canadian men who held this position were highly respected and committed to the success of the Black community.

CHAIRMEN OF EMANCIPATION DAY CELEBRATIONS

Dr. Daniel Pierson officiated Emancipation Day in Amherstburg for about seven years between 1884 to 1893. A practising physician in Amherstburg, he learned medicine while enslaved in the state of Kentucky.[5]

Delos Rogest Davis, a lawyer, was the master of ceremonies in Amherstburg in 1894. In 1885 this son of a former slave had become the second Black lawyer in Canada.

William H. Bazie, AME pastor, was chairman of the day in Chatham, both in 1889 and 1899.

Thomas Smallwood was president of the day at Toronto's twentieth anniversary of Emancipation Day, in 1854. He was a freedom seeker. Thomas operated a saw factory, and he wrote his autobiography, *A Narrative of Thomas Smallwood (Coloured Man)*, in 1851. It was the first slave narrative to be written and published in Canada.

George Morton presided over the day's exercises in Hamilton in 1884. George was born in Hamilton and delivered mail for thirty-six years after leaving his job as a barber. He was active in several Black organizations in his community, including the Brotherly Union Society and the Mount Brydges Lodge No. 1865.

Bertrand Joseph Spencer Pitt was a Toronto lawyer who managed the "Big Picnic" in St. Catharines from 1924 to 1951.

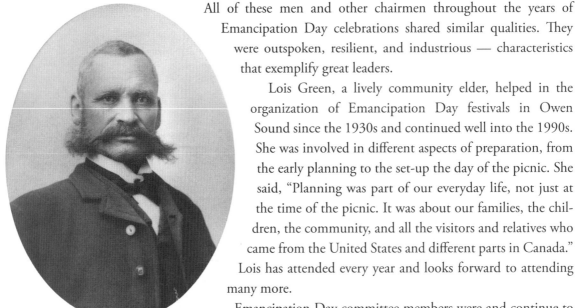

Henry Weaver. A park located across the street from the site of his grocery store on Duke Street was dedicated in honour of Henry Weaver's contributions to Chatham.

Courtesy of the Chatham-Kent Museum. 1999-52-11.

All of these men and other chairmen throughout the years of Emancipation Day celebrations shared similar qualities. They were outspoken, resilient, and industrious — characteristics that exemplify great leaders.

Lois Green, a lively community elder, helped in the organization of Emancipation Day festivals in Owen Sound since the 1930s and continued well into the 1990s. She was involved in different aspects of preparation, from the early planning to the set-up the day of the picnic. She said, "Planning was part of our everyday life, not just at the time of the picnic. It was about our families, the children, the community, and all the visitors and relatives who came from the United States and different parts in Canada." Lois has attended every year and looks forward to attending many more.

Emancipation Day committee members were and continue to be skilled, dedicated volunteers representing a cross-section of African-Canadian society. Time and time again, they demonstrate their ability to organize parades, volunteers, and ensure successful celebrations.

Bertrand Joseph Spencer Pitt is decorated with an official UNIA Emancipation Day committee ribbon by his wife Mary Pitt while their three children, Spencer, 10, and twins Mary and Franklin, 8, proudly watch. His law office was located on Dundas Street in Toronto. Pitt is remembered as a mentor for young Black lawyers and an advocate of equal rights.

From the *St. Catharines Standard*, August 6, 1954. *Courtesy of the St. Catharines Museum, Standard Collection, S1954.17.10.1.*

CHAPTER FOUR

THE CELEBRANTS: COME ONE, COME ALL

When every heart joins every heart and together yearns for liberty,
that's when we'll be free.
— "Hymn to Freedom," Oscar Peterson, *Night Train*, 1962

In Canada all kinds of people observed the abolition of British slavery: Canadian-born Blacks, some the descendants of local slaves; Black Loyalists and their descendants; free Blacks; and fugitive slaves from the United States. They were uneducated or professionals, small-town residents and urban dwellers, and were from all facets of society and all ages. Emancipation Day was also celebrated by people from diverse racial, ethnic, and religious groups. Hundreds of these individuals, out-of-town guests from surrounding towns and nearby American centres, along with Native and White community members, celebrated African liberation throughout Ontario. They travelled by foot, horse and wagon, train, passenger steamboats, electric streetcars, and automobiles.

WHAT THEY WERE SAYING

"By automobile, bus, train, and even horse and buggy colored residents from different parts of Canada and the United States drifted into Windsor today to celebrate the 97th anniversary of Emancipation. Farmers from colored communities in Essex County used the horse and buggy as their means of transportation."

— *Owen Sound Daily Sun Times*, August 1, 1935.

"The ferry boats and incoming trains brought in the usual representation of the colored race."

— *Windsor Evening Record*, August 1, 1912.

"Hundreds of men and women of color went to the park in automobiles, gaudy with streamers and driven by white chauffeurs."

— *Windsor Evening Record*, August 2, 1913.

"They came by steamboats, by rail and in buggies and wagons."

— *Windsor Evening Record*, August 1, 1893.

"By automobile, bus, train and horse and buggy negroes from many sections of Canada and the United States came here to-day to celebrate the anniversary of emancipation."

— *Toronto Star*, August 1, 1935.

DESCENDANTS OF ENSLAVED AFRICAN CANADIANS

Contrary to what many believe, slavery was practised right here in Canada for over two hundred years! People of African descent were enslaved in Canada as early as 1628 in the Maritime provinces of Nova Scotia, New Brunswick, and Prince Edward Island, historically known as Acadia. Other French settlements where Africans were enslaved included Île Royale (Cape Breton Island), Montreal, and various Quebec towns. Natives were also enslaved by the French in New France.

Enslaved Africans came to Canada as the property of their United Empire Loyalist masters, starting in 1783. This was after the British defeat in the American Revolutionary War saw the Patriots succeed in breaking away from Britain to form their own country, the United States of America. These slaves were used to fill the labour shortage in the developing colonies.

Enslaved Africans were imported from the Caribbean, Europe, and the United States into Canada as the personal property of Whites coming to live in Canada or as investment goods to be sold for profit. They were auctioned off in regular markets in many Canadian towns, in the same places where people would go to buy bread, fruits, and vegetables. Slaves were also sold privately, bequeathed in wills, and given as gifts. European settlers from all levels of society — church clergy, military officers, farmers, merchants, and government officials — owned enslaved Africans.

Generations of people of African origin were enslaved in Canada. They settled in many villages, towns, and urban centres in the Maritimes, Quebec, and Ontario, and were held in bondage until the 1793 Act to Limit Slavery in Upper Canada became law. It gradually abolished slavery in Upper Canada (now Ontario). Those enslaved in 1793 would remain in bondage until death or until they were freed by their owners. Their children would be freed at the age of twenty-five, and any children born to them would be free at birth.

In the 1780s, John Baker was born enslaved in Montreal. He was the son of an enslaved woman named Dorinda (or Dorine) Baker. Dorinda, John, and his brother Simon were the property of Robert Isaac Dey Gray, solicitor general of Upper Canada. However, his sisters — one we know was named Elizabeth — seemed to have been born free due to the 1793 Act to Limit Slavery in Upper Canada. They eventually settled in York, now known as the city of Toronto. The enslaved family members were freed by Mr. Gray's will in 1804. John enlisted in the 104th (New Brunswick) Regiment of Foot of the British Army. He fought in the War of 1812 in the battle at Sackets Harbor, New York, in May 1813; the Battle of Lundy's Lane in Niagara on July 25, 1814; and the two-month Siege of Fort Erie during the summer of 1814. He then went overseas and fought in the Battle of Waterloo, which is now Belgium. When, in 1817, John was discharged in Montreal, he moved to Oshawa, Ontario, to live on

WHAT THEY WERE SAYING

John baker, a colored man, died at Cornwall on the 18th inst. He celebrated his one hundred and fifth birth-day on last Christmas Day. Baker came to Cornwall a Slave to the late Colonel Grey in 1792: he Had then seen service in the Revolutionary War. He subsequently served through the war of 1812 and was wounded at Lundy's Lane. He has drawn a pension for 57 years. Baker retained his faculties till the last and was walking in the street less than three weeks ago. He took particular delight in naming over the British Sovereigns whom he had served under and spinning yarns. he was buried with military honors.

— Freeholder

the 200 acres of land given to him by his former master. John Baker was in his nineties when he died, on January 18, 1871. Prior to being freed, he was the last surviving enslaved Black person in Ontario and Quebec.

Also enslaved were Peggy and her children, Jupiter, Milly, and Amy. They were owned by Peter Russell, the receiver general of Upper Canada, and his sister, Elizabeth Russell. Peggy worked as the cook and washerwoman. Peggy's husband, Pompadour, was a free Black who worked on the Russell farm in Toronto. Jupiter was employed as a house servant and farmhand. In February 1806, Peggy and Jupiter were advertised for sale in a newspaper by the Russells because they found them to be quite unmanageable. In several instances, Peggy ran away for short periods of times, and Jupiter was described as defiant — he was jailed for a number of offences. This level of "disobedience" was common for slaves as a form of resistance. Miss Russell inherited her brother's property, including the slaves, when he died in 1808. Shortly after, Elizabeth Russell gave Amy to her goddaughter, Elizabeth Denison, as a gift. The only known descendant of the Pompadour family is Amy's son, Duke Denison, who was born in 1811 and was said to have lived until the mid-1800s.[1] Nothing further is known about the Pompadour family.

Hank and Sukey appear to be two of the last of enslaved Africans in Canada. Prominent lawyer Sir Adam Wilson saw the young boy and young girl working in the home of Mrs. Deborah O'Reilly — mother of Queen's Council and lawyer Miles O'Reilly — in Halton County, Ontario, just before the Slavery Abolition Act came in to effect in 1834. They were subsequently freed.[2]

Nancy Morton, Marie-Joseph Angélique, Marie Marguerite Rose, Sam Martin, and Henry Lewis are just a handful of the known names of the approximately 1,500 of Black people enslaved in eastern Canadian provinces for over two centuries. The practice was completely eradicated in the British colonies in 1834 by the British Parliament's passage of the Slavery Abolition Act. In the United States, however, slavery was alive and well.

FUGITIVE AMERICAN SLAVES

In their quest for freedom, enslaved African Americans began migrating to Canada immediately after the War of 1812. British legislation made Canada attractive to runaways because the 1793 Act to Limit Slavery automatically freed any fugitives coming in to Upper Canada, and the 1833 Slavery Abolition Act ended the practice of slavery on Canadian soil. That meant that all Blacks were free north of the American border. The first wave came mainly from the Chesapeake area to Nova Scotia and other Maritime provinces. Ex-slave Reverend Richard Preston, for example, settled in Halifax, Nova Scotia, in 1816. Robert Whetsel, also a fugitive slave, settled in Saint John, New Brunswick, in 1852.

After the War of 1812, word spread from American soldiers that they had fought free "Black men in red coats" in Upper Canada, beginning the northward migration of African-American fugitives. The majority settled in Canada West (Ontario). In the 1820s, fugitives continued to escape from southern states to communities in Ontario with large Black populations. Some who fled used the secret escape network of anti-slavery sympathisers, called the Underground Railroad (UGRR). The UGRR operated on land and across waterways, helping escapees from southern states to reach northern free states, or to travel even farther north to freedom in Canada. "Stations" in Canada included Chatham, Dresden, Buxton, Sandwich, Amherstburg, and Owen Sound, which was the most northerly terminal on the UGRR.

Those who used the UGRR escaped from the United States with the assistance of Black and White abolitionists, which including Quakers of the Society of Friends, clergymen from various Christian denominations, and Native Americans. Freedom seekers used secret routes through Detroit, Niagara, or Ohio after passing through states such as Pennsylvania, New York, Vermont, Maine, and Indiana. Once they arrived at the Canada-United States border — after an

SPOTLIGHT ON ...

Richard Preston escaped from slavery as a young boy and settled in Nova Scotia. He was an anti-slavery activist and a community leader. In 1846 Preston founded the African Abolition Society, which organized Emancipation Day celebrations in Halifax for at least twelve years. He established eleven Baptist churches in Nova Scotia and organized the African Baptist Association of Nova Scotia.

arduous and frightening journey — many made the final escape to free Canadian soil on cargo vessels, steamers, or small boats crossing Lake Erie, the Detroit River, and the Lower Niagara River. Others walked across frozen rivers to free land, or were transported by horse-drawn wagons, ferry boats, and trains.

Former escapees risked their lives and newfound liberty to help lead fellow fugitives to Canada. For example, Harriet Tubman, known as "the Moses of her people," was a famous conductor of the UGRR who worked out of St. Catharines for eight years, and James Wesley Hill, nicknamed "Canada Jim," operated an Oakville depot for runaways. Both made secret trips into the United States to bring fugitives into Canada. However, many enslaved African Americans escaped without any help.

Several instances of slaves escaping from the United States to Canada raised legal challenges. Slave owners often asked for the return of their "property" — fugitives who sought freedom in Canada. In Upper Canada's response to an 1819 extradition request, John Beverley Johnson declared, "... whatever may have been the condition of the Negroes in the Country to which they formerly belonged, here they are free — For the enjoyment of all civil rights and ... and among them the right to personal freedom as acknowledged and protected by the Laws of England ..."[3] Subsequent fugitive extradition cases included Thornton and Lucie Blackburn, 1833; Jesse Happy and Solomon Moseby, 1837; Nelson Hackett, 1841; and John Anderson, 1860. The freedom of all but one of these fugitives who escaped to Canada was upheld by the courts. Solomon Moseby was ordered to be returned to his master in Kentucky, but he was able to escape when a riot over his transfer took place.

When the 1850 Fugitive Slave Act became law in America, a flood of runaways arrived in Canada. Under this regulation, which

---

SPOTLIGHT ON ...

Virginia fugitive Robert Whetsel settled in Saint John, New Brunswick, around 1852. He operated several businesses, including a barbershop, an oyster saloon, and the only ice business in the city. Whetsel was very involved in Saint John's Black community. He delivered a speech and was the chairman for the 1863 Emancipation Day observance that was attended by Blacks and Whites.

THE CELEBRANTS: COME ONE, COME ALL

was harsher than the 1793 version, fugitives slaves could be caught and sent back into slavery from northern states. It enforced the rights of slave owners, making it mandatory for those even in free northern states to assist in the recapture of escapees, with harsh punishment such as large fines or jail time for those who helped slaves run away. The 1850 Fugitive Slave Act also gave slave owners and the bounty hunters who worked for them the power to track and capture fugitives anywhere in America. It also required local law enforcers to assist in returning such people to bondage by arresting and taking them into custody. Rewards were offered to encourage others to aid in recapturing fugitives. The result of this law was that some runaways and free Blacks were captured and sent into slavery down south. Therefore, no Black person, either free or enslaved, was safe. The situation triggered a mass flight of American refugees to Canada. By the end of the 1850s, approximately 50,000 freedom seekers had made Canada their new home.

Once in Canada, many fugitives received support from the communities they were starting their new lives in. Churches of all denominations established missions to help refugees settle. These missions offered places of worship, food, clothing, temporary shelter, employment assistance, and schooling. Some settlements were created specifically for fugitives. The Dawn Settlement, located near Dresden, Ontario, was founded in 1842 by Reverends Josiah Henson and Hiram Wilson. The Wilberforce settlement in Lucan, just north of London, Ontario, was the first planned settlement for Blacks in the 1830s. It was organized by a group of African Americans in Cincinnati, Ohio, with the help of Quakers in Ohio and Indiana.

TRACING THE UNDERGROUND RAILROAD

In 2012 Owen Sound will recognize 150 years of continuous commemoration of Emancipation Day. Plans are well underway with the return of the "Adventure Cyclists," who ride their bicycles through the United States, tracing one of the Underground Railroad routes taken by fugitives on their way to Canada. An Ancestor's Breakfast will be hosted at Harrison Park and an interactive Underground Railroad journey for youth. There will also be a parade from Harrison Park to Kelso Beach for the Emancipation festival's Saturday afternoon activities, which will be capped with their largest musical presentation ever.

Oro was the only government-sponsored settlement for Blacks, and it was set up by the lieutenant governor of Upper Canada, Sir Peregrine Maitland, in 1819. The community was situated northwest of Barrie in Simcoe County. The Elgin Settlement was in present-day Buxton, which is just south of Chatham, in southwestern Ontario. It was started by Reverend William King in 1849. They cleared land, built homes, and established many important community institutions. The freedom, opportunity, and prospects that Canada represented to runaways were grounds for joyous celebration.

DESCENDANTS OF FUGITIVES

The early descendants of fugitives either arrived from the United States at a very young age with their escaping family or were born in Canada. They continued homesteading, obtained an education, and many relocated to other parts of the province in search of better opportunities. Collectively, they have contributed to the historical, economic, and cultural development of Canada.

First generation descendants celebrated Emancipation Day with as much enthusiasm as their older family members. Peter Gallego, who attended Upper Canada College and graduated from the University of Toronto, was very active in Toronto's Black community in the 1830s and 1840s. He was the son of a former slave from Richmond, Virginia, who wanted to travel to Africa to do missionary work. In Toronto he collected statistics on the number of African Canadians in the city. Gallego was also an officer of the British-American Anti-Slavery Society. William Henry Smallwood also attended Upper Canada College in the 1850s. His father was a fugitive slave from Maryland who operated a saw factory on Front Street in Toronto and played a role in organizing Emancipation Day.

SPOTLIGHT ON ...

The Aylestock family were descendants of early Blacks who settled in Wellington and Waterloo Counties along the Conestogo River, an area known as the Queen's Bush settlement. Addie Aylestock was the first Black woman to be ordained in the BME church and as a church minister in Canada. Her sister Rella Braithwaite (née Aylestock) authored several books on African-Canadian history. Rella's daughter is Diana Braithwaite, a renowned jazz and blues singer.

Amherstburg school principal John Henry Alexander regularly participated in the special occasion. John Henry's father, Thomas Alexander, was a fugitive slave who escaped from a plantation in Kentucky and settled in Anderdon Township, north of Amherstburg, in the 1840s. John and his wife had six children. He was a town councillor from 1923 to 1926 and was later appointed as Amherstburg's Town Assessor in 1930. Another first generation descendent, church minister Josephus O'Banyoun, was born and raised in Brantford, Ontario. His father, Peter Simeon O'Banyoun, was a runaway slave from Kentucky. Josephus was involved in many aspects of community life, including Emancipation Day.

In a unique story, John Lindsay was born free in 1806, but was kidnapped and sold into slavery at the age of seven. The experienced blacksmith remained enslaved until he ran away to Canada in 1835 and decided to live in St. Catharines. John immediately began to participate in his new community and even offered a celebratory toast at that year's Emancipation Day gathering, held at the AME church. He went on to have a family and expanded his career into teaching, gardening, and operating a brewery.[4]

Second, third, fourth, and fifth generation Canadians continued to recognize August First:

- The Alexander and Johnson families in Amherstburg

- The Allen family in Windsor

- The Aylestock family in Glen Allan, formerly part of the Queen's Bush area

- Descendants of Josiah Henson

- The Prince family in Chatham-Kent County

- The Perrys of Windsor

- The Bell and Harper families in St. Catharines

- The Duncan family in Oakville

- The Green, Scott, and Miller families in Owen Sound.

- The Walls family of Puce (now Lakeshore, Ontario, near Windsor)

Descendants of these families assisted in the organization of the commemoration and were part of the programmes. They marked the anniversary of the abolition of slavery with family, friends, and visitors. To this day, members of the Scott and Allen families are involved in the celebration.

FREE BLACKS

Free Blacks were people who were not born into slavery. They were free persons who had some rights, but by the 1840s, their everyday lives were becoming more restricted and their freedom was in jeopardy. This was especially true after the passage of the Fugitive Slave Act of 1850. Free Blacks were required to carry papers, familiarly known as freedom papers, to prove they were "free persons of colour" and not slaves. This important piece of paper recorded personal information of the carrier. It served as a guarantee of the free persons' status in the event that bounty hunters tried to pick them up. Sometimes they had to put up a large amount of money as security for their freedom. Some free Blacks could not vote or own property in certain northern towns. As a result of the Fugitive Slave Act bringing more bounty hunters to the north, many free Blacks were kidnapped and returned to slavery in the South. So, in the mid-nineteenth century, large numbers of free African Americans migrated mainly from the northern United States like New York and Ohio and settled across Ontario and eastern Canada, where they lived productive lives and assisted in the development of Black communities.

Newly arrived immigrants included members of the Shadd clan, which consisted of Abraham Doras Shadd, his wife Harriet, and his children Mary Ann Shadd (later Cary), Garrison Shadd, and Isaac Shadd. They all came from

Delaware and Pennsylvania and settled in Windsor, Buxton, and Chatham. While living in the United States, the abolitionist family helped runaways find their way to freedom. Abraham and Harriet opened a school on their property in North Buxton to provide an education to fugitives young and old. Abraham, who was a shoemaker by profession, became the first Black politician in Canada when he was elected to the Raleigh Township city council in 1859.

The Cary brothers — George W., Thomas F. (Mary Ann Shadd's husband), and Isaac N. — were "... strong abolitionists. They campaigned against racial prejudice, led Black self-help organizations, organized Black conventions, and urged the city's Blacks to abandon the Conservative Party and support George Brown's Reform Party or the Liberals."[5]

Wilson Ruffin Abbott and his wife, Ellen Toyer Abbott, were both born free. Wilson was born in Richmond, Virginia, and Ellen in Boston, Massachusetts. They were forced to leave a successful grocery business in Mobile, Alabama, because of the increasing discrimination against African Americans. The Abbotts and their three surviving children, including doctor Anderson Ruffin Abbott, lived in Toronto — Anderson was the first Canadian-born Black to become a medical doctor.

In Toronto Wilson became a wealthy real estate holder, owning properties in Toronto, Hamilton, and Owen Sound. Wilson and Ellen were committed to the growth and improvement of the Black community. Through various benevolent organizations, they provided assistance to fugitive slaves in Toronto. Ellen was the president of the Queen Victoria Benevolent Society. Wilson was a founding member of the Anti-Slavery Society of Canada and the Coloured Wesleyan Methodist Church. He served in the militia that protected Toronto during the Rebellions of 1837–38 and was elected to the Toronto city council in 1840.

Prominent doctor and abolitionist Martin R. Delany was one of the featured speakers at Emancipation Day commemorations in Chatham in 1857. The physician and his wife Catherine moved to Chatham in 1856 from Pittsburgh, Pennsylvania. Immediately after his arrival, Martin helped to mobilize Black voters in the county to vote for reformer and member of Parliament Archibald McKellar in the 1856 provincial election. As an abolitionist, he travelled to speak out against American slavery and wrote articles in various publications to express his views. Martin returned to the United States in 1865 as a recruitment officer for the Civil War, and one month after his return was made a major and army doctor in the Union Army.

Branson Johnson, his wife Amanda, and their three children emigrated from Maryland and settled Oakville in the early 1860s. Their family grew to seven children. Branson was an active member of the AME church and worked as a railway porter.

Canadian-born descendants of free Blacks who migrated to Canada maintained the annual commemoration August First in the twentieth century and continue to do so in the twenty-first. Anderson Ruffin Abbott's memory of attending an Emancipation Day as a young man in the 1850s was recorded:

> On one occasion within my memory they provided a banquet which was held under a pavilion erected on a vacant lot running from Elizabeth Street to Sayre Street opposite Osgoode Hall, which was then a barracks for the [32nd] West India Regiment. The procession was headed by the band of the Regiment. The tallest man in this Regiment was a Black man, a drummer, known as Black Charlie. The procession carried a Union Jack and a blue silk banner on which was inscribed in glit letters "The Abolition Society, Organized 1844." The mayor of the city, Mr. Metcalfe, made a speech … followed by several other speeches of prominent citizens. These celebrations were carried on yearly amid much enthusiasm, because it gave the refugee colonists an opportunity to express their gratitude and appreciation of the privileges they enjoyed under British rule.[6]

His recollection provides valuable historical insight into early celebrations.

Robert Leonard Dunn delivered several speeches. Brothers Robert and James Llewlyn Dunn were born in St. Thomas, Ontario, south of London and moved to Windsor, where they became well-known and successful. James and Robert co-owned and operated the Standard Paint and Varnish Company. Robert also owned a theatre in Detroit, Michigan, with other business partners. In 1887 James became the first African-Canadian city councillor of Windsor and was voted into office again in 1888.[7] Robert also entered local politics as an alderman in 1893 and served seven terms. Both men were members of the BME church and the Windsor lodge of the Grand United Order of Oddfellows.[8]

Historian, author, curator Adrienne Shadd is a descendant of the original Shadd settlers. As a young girl she participated in the festival in Windsor, and has

Robert L. Dunn (right) and James L. Dunn (left).

Courtesy of the E. Andrea Shreve Moore Collection, Essex County Black Historical Research Society.

more recently shared her wealth of knowledge on African-Canadian history at Emancipation Day events as a guest speaker. In 2009 she received the Toronto Equity and Human Rights Award.

All of these people are still just a few of those who preserved the tradition of celebrating freedom.

AFRICAN CANADIAN SOLDIERS

Black men have served in every major British war in North America. During the American Revolutionary War (1775–1783), Black Loyalists included free Blacks and former slaves who fought for Britain. Behind British lines they worked as soldiers, cooks, laundry workers, general labourers, shoemakers, musicians, tailors, construction workers, and ship advisors to the ship master, who helped to navigate ships in and out of harbours and through congested or dangerous waters. After the war, the Black Loyalists who were declared free were transported to Canada, mainly to Nova Scotia, while the Black Loyalists who came to Upper and Lower Canada were generally enslaved, property of their White Loyalist masters. They fought alongside their owners. With few exceptions, they were not granted freedom or land for their military service to the British crown as was promised. Loyalists began arriving in Canada in 1783, once British defeat was inevitable. Butler's Rangers, a militia including men such as Richard Pierpoint, John Vanpatten, James Robertson, and Robert Jupiter, fought under Loyalist Lieutenant Colonel John Butler in several battles in Ohio, Pennsylvania, Michigan, Virginia, and Kentucky. They were based at Fort Niagara in northern New York, which is located on the shore of Lake Ontario at the mouth of the Niagara River. The names of three thousand Black Loyalists are recorded in the Book of Negroes.

BOOK OF NEGROES

The Book of Negroes is a 150-page military ledger that included the names of 3,000 Black Loyalists. It was the first major record of people of African descent in North America. In 1783 these Black passengers were leaving the port of Manhattan, New York, sailing on the Hudson River to eastern Canada. Some were free, some were indentured servants, and some were the enslaved property of British officers. The handwritten entries of each person included name, age, a brief description of their physical appearance, life circumstances, and their status — free or slave. The people in this document were some of the thousands of Blacks, the majority enslaved, who responded to the British call for Blacks to leave their slave masters and take up arms in support of the British offence in the American Revolution. In return for their service they were promised freedom and protection by the British. Black men and women served as soldiers, labourers, cooks, and in other roles. In the end, as part of the peace accord with the Americans that was signed in Paris in 1782, Britain agreed not to take "any Negroes or other property of the American Inhabitants." So, unfortunately, some African Americans did not escape bondage in the United States, because the British had to determine the eligibility of freedom based on those who joined the British prior to the signing of the treaty and those who served behind British lines for at least one year. After being registered in the ledger and receiving a passenger ticket aboard a ship, some were transported overseas to England and Germany. Most were transported to Canada, where some landed in Quebec, but the majority settled in Nova Scotia in towns like Halifax, Shelburne, and Annapolis Royal.

Black soldiers also protected British and Canadian interests in other conflicts. Coloured corps, which were racially segregated military units, were formed by men of African descent during the War of 1812, the Rebellions of 1837–38, and the First World War. For example, Runchey's Coloured Corps under the command of Captain Robert Runchey, based at Fort George in Niagara-on-the-Lake, fought in the War of 1812. During the rebellions of 1837–38, several coloured corps were raised to secure the borders, including the 1st and 2nd Coloured Corps from Chatham and Windsor area, under Captain Caldwell and

African-Canadian men from across Canada enlisted and served in the No. 2 Construction Battalion, Canadian Expeditionary Force.

Courtesy of the Black Cultural Centre of Nova Scotia.

Josiah Henson; the Coloured Corps of Upper Canada in the Niagara region; and the Toronto Coloured Corps, led by Colonel Samuel Jarvis, son of William Jarvis.

During the middle of the First World War, Black volunteer militiamen were allowed to serve as non-combat troops in the No. 2 Construction Battalion, raised in 1916. The construction unit's duties included building roads and bridges, defusing land mines, logging, shipping, and milling. Later, Black men were able to enlist in racially integrated units in the Second World War. They fought to preserve the freedom guaranteed to them and other African Canadians under the British flag. The Toronto Veterans Colour Guard honoured the lives and contributions of Black soldiers at Emancipation Day observances in Toronto in the 1950s and 1960s. Wreaths were laid on the memorial cenotaph at Victoria Memorial Park. However, their own country was another battleground in the fight for freedom. These brave war veterans and their courageous sons, who followed in their footsteps, marched proudly in Emancipation Day parades and the attendees rightfully paid homage to them.

WEST INDIAN IMMIGRANTS AND THEIR DESCENDANTS

West Indians entered Canada in different waves of immigration. Approximately six hundred Jamaican Maroons came to Nova Scotia in 1796. They were deported from Jamaica because of their rebellion against the ruling British colonial government. The Maroons were provided with settlement land in the Preston area of Nova Scotia, and a number of today's Black population in Nova Scotia are their descendants. The Maroons were instrumental in constructing one of the defence walls on Citadel Hill in Halifax and helped to build Government House, home of the lieutenant-governor and the first official government residence in Canada. Aside from these high-profile projects, they worked in other jobs as manual labourers.

Between 1800 and 1920, men from Jamaica and Barbados came to work in the mines in Cape Breton and Sydney, Nova Scotia. Gold prospectors like Jamaican John Robert Giscome and Bahamian Henry McDame arrived in British Columbia in 1858 during the gold rush.

This trend in immigration continued, with hundreds of West Indian men and women coming to Canada to attend universities and later deciding not to return to the West Indies. A good example of this is Jamaican-born Robert Sutherland, the first Black lawyer in Canada. He practised law in Kitchener (then called Berlin) and Walkerton, Ontario, south of Owen Sound area. Robert came to Canada in 1849 to study classical studies and mathematics at Queen's University. After graduating, Sutherland went to Toronto to study law at Osgoode Hall and was called to the bar in 1855. When he died of pneumonia in 1878, he left his entire estate worth $12,000 to Queen's University, which was the largest donation to the university up to that time.

Bertrand Joseph Spencer Pitt, another man who immigrated to study, was from Grenada. He arrived in Nova Scotia in the early 1920s to attend the law program at Dalhousie University. Pitt was the fifth Black lawyer of Ontario. He played a leading role in the organization of St. Catharine's "Big Picnic" Emancipation Day celebrations from 1924 to 1951 in his capacity as president and lawyer for the Toronto branch of the Universal Negro Improvement Association.

In the 1950s and 1960s, more Blacks continued to arrive from Commonwealth Caribbean countries — former British colonies — as university students, entrepreneurs, and job seekers. Donald Moore emigrated from Barbados in 1913. He started a tailoring business in Toronto and was a specialist in the local textile industry. Donald was very active in the Black community and tirelessly advocated for the fair treatment of African Canadians and other minorities. He was also the head of the Toronto Emancipation Committee, the organization that sponsored Emancipation Day commemorations in the 1950s and 1960s.

The West Indian Domestic Scheme, a government immigration program that ran from 1955 to 1960, recruited Black women from the Caribbean to move to Canada to work as domestic servants in White households. In their native islands, these women were mainly teachers, office workers, and nurses. By 1965 almost three thousand women were admitted to work as household maids for a minimum of one year, after which they received landed immigrant status and could sponsor family members.

The Honourable Jean Augustine came to Canada from Grenada in 1960 under the Domestic Scheme. Although she was a trained teacher, Jean worked as a domestic, as required by the program, in various jobs while pursuing a university degree. She became an elementary school teacher and principal in Toronto before entering federal politics. In 1993 she was elected as a Liberal member of Parliament — the first Black woman in Canadian history to achieve this. Jean introduced a bill in the House of Commons in 1995 to have Black History Month declared an official commemoration, provincially and nationally. It was approved by all political parties. Jean accomplished another first: her appointment as the first fairness commissioner for Ontario, in 2007, and in 2009 was the first Grenadian-born to be a recipient of the Order of Canada. In 2009 Jean was the keynote speaker for the opening gala of the Emancipation Day celebrations, revived by the Windsor Emancipation Celebration Corporation.

Another notable achiever was Ovid Jackson, Owen Sound's first Black mayor — in office from 1983 to 1993 — and Order of Canada recipient. He was born in Guyana and emigrated to Canada in 1966, initially working as a mechanic and later a teacher. Jackson was elected as a city councillor, an office he held from 1974 to 1982. He was then voted as mayor of Owen Sound in 1983 and held this position until 1993, when he entered federal politics. Ovid was the member of Parliament for the Liberal Party of Bruce-Grey-Owen Sound, from 1994 to 2004. He was the featured speaker when Emancipation Day commemorations returned to Amherstburg in 1983, and in 2010 Ovid was honoured at the Emancipation Festival in Owen Sound for his contributions to and accomplishments in the region's Black history.

Like the men and women mentioned, many more newly-arrived made the cities of Toronto, Hamilton, London, Montreal, and Windsor their home and contributed immensely to the development of various Black communities and the country.

West Indians were coming from countries where thousands of enslaved Africans were freed by the Slavery Abolition Act of 1833 and commemorated Emancipation Day. The incoming residents carried on the tradition in the customary way, but also brought with them a manner of celebration new to Canadians. Caribana was established in 1967 by a group of West Indian immigrants who settled in Toronto. With its beginnings in the carnival of Trinidad, the forty-three year old festival includes a big, colourful street parade and illustrates a Caribbean style of celebrating Emancipation Day. Today, Caribana attracts over one million people every year and is one of the largest street festivals in North America. The grand procession and associated events generate an estimated five hundred million dollars for the local economy of Toronto every year.

Descendants of West Indian immigrants continued to lead productive lives and make invaluable contributions to their communities in Canada. Countless descendants went on to achieve extraordinary success. One notable case is the Honourable Lincoln Alexander, born in Toronto in 1922. His mother was Jamaican and his father was from St. Vincent and the Grenadines. Respectively, they worked as a domestic helper and a railway porter to support their family. Lincoln served in the Royal Canadian Air Force in the Second World War. After the war, he became a respected lawyer and politician. Lincoln made history by earning the distinctions of Canada's first Black member of Parliament, first Black federal cabinet minister, and Ontario's first Black lieutenant governor.

Stanley Grizzle was born in Toronto in 1918 to Jamaican parents. He served in the Second World War. When he returned to Canada, he was employed as a train porter and active in the labour and human rights movement through his extensive involvement with the Brotherhood of Sleeping Car Porters. In 1978 Stanley became the first African-Canadian Citizenship Court judge. He was awarded the Order of Canada for his extraordinary community work. Stanley attended Emancipation Day observances in Toronto with his family during the 1950s and 1960s and also addressed the audiences there.

The outstanding achievements of West Indian expatriates and their descendants have been important to the development of Canada. They played a vital role in affecting social change, especially during the civil rights and labour movements. Their involvement in Emancipation Day — or West India Day, as it was popularly known — in Canada continues to hold historical significance for them. Their participation helped to maintain its significance as an international public observance, while influencing the evolution of the commemoration.

WHITES

Numerous Emancipation Day celebrants were European Canadians. During the first fifty years of commemorations, the Whites that attended August First commemorations were sympathetic Whites — people who supported the cause of freedom and equality for those of African descent. White abolitionists believed slavery was wrong, and some assisted in bringing fugitives to freedom in Canada. For the first three decades until the end of American slavery, White abolitionists were active in pushing for human rights for Blacks and the end of slavery. They believed that no human being should own the life of another and that Blacks were entitled to the same rights as all other Canadians. They worked together with Black leaders and organizations to raise money meant to help fugitives and provide settlement support such as shelter, food, clothing, education, and jobs to entering refugees. They also formed and joined anti-slavery societies to influence the public's view on slavery and push for American and Canadian legislation against it.

The Anti-Slavery Society of Canada (ASSC) was created in 1851, with its headquarters in Toronto. It was established by George Brown, a Father of Confederation and the publisher of the *Globe* newspaper, along with both Black and White associates in Ontario and Quebec. White members included Dr. Michael Willis, principal of Knox College, University of Toronto; Reverend William McClure of London, Ontario; Captain Charles Stuart, former army major who worked with fugitives in Amherstburg; Oliver Mowat, politician and third premier of Ontario; and newspaper editor John Dougall of Montreal. Black members of the ASSC included African-American abolitionist and short-term Upper Canada resident Samuel Ringgold Ward, who was a fugitive from Maryland; businessman Wilson Ruffin Abbott of Toronto; and entrepreneur Aby Beckford Jones of London, Ontario.

George Brown and John Dougall, publisher of the *Montreal Gazette*, used their papers to criticize the practice of slavery in the South, discuss issues facing arriving fugitives, and share accounts of annual Emancipation Day celebrations across the country. For their part, the wives of the White members of the ASSC formed the Ladies Association for the Relief of Colored Destitute Fugitives to also assist in providing help to Black refugees.

Many of the White participants in the early years were church ministers of various denominations. They delivered sermons or speeches at Emancipation Day events, and some even played a role in the overall organization of the festivities:

> **William King** was a Presbyterian minister who founded the Elgin Settlement in Buxton for fugitive slaves. He spoke at several gatherings in Chatham.

Marmaduke Martin Dillon, an Anglican priest in London, worked as a missionary to the fugitive slaves in the city and conducted an Emancipation Day service in 1855 at St. Paul's Church.

John Gamble Geddes delivered a sermon at Christ's Church Cathedral in Hamilton in 1846 and again in 1857.

Charles Henry Drinkwater, also in Hamilton, opened the doors of St. Thomas Church to celebrants in 1864. His sermon and the proceedings of the day were published, quite likely to be sold to raise money for local organizations that supported fugitive slaves.

Henry James Grasett, the rector of St. James Cathedral from 1842 to 1847, addressed numerous crowds for over twenty years, beginning in 1839. This church was a regular meeting place in Toronto.

Thomas Hughes, of Christ's Church Anglican, went to Dresden in 1859 to work with fugitive slaves. Thomas supervised the mission school that was established by the Anglican Church. Once summer exams were finished in 1861, he hosted an Emancipation Day assembly for students in a field on his property. In an entry in his diary dated August 1, 1861, Thomas describes how local African Canadians came to enjoy the picnic.

The Fraser River Gold Rush in British Columbia saw many Black settlers arrive in the hopes of building a new life, and William F. Clarke was very active in assisting incoming African Americans to settle in their new country. The Congregationalist minister had originally worked with fugitive slaves in Norwich and London in Canada West before going to Victoria, British Columbia, in 1857

Reverend William F. Clarke.

Courtesy of the University of Guelph Library, Archival and Special Collections.

Reverend William McClure was referred to by African-American abolitionist Samuel Ringgold Ward "as true a friend to the negro as ever drew breath."

From the *Life and Labours of the Reverend William McClure.*

The Honourable Isaac Buchanan, MPP for Hamilton, Canada West (1857–1865), lent the grounds of his Clairmont Park estate on Hamilton Mountain for annual Emancipation Day celebrations in that city. He also supported efforts that improved the rights and opportunities for local African Canadians.

to assist the large wave of settlers that the promise of gold had brought. The wave included approximately eight hundred Black men and women from San Francisco, California, and Clarke welcomed them into the church, refusing to establish a segregated section. William was also a founder of the London branch of the ASSC, along with William McClure, minister of the Irish New Connexion Methodist Chapel, and Black businessman and resident Aby Beckford Jones. Both Williams delivered speeches at the 1852 celebration in London.

White politicians — mayors, city councillors, members of Parliament (MPs), and members of Provincial Parliament (MPPs) — regularly attended August First events, officially welcoming guests and delivering speeches. Participating in Emancipation Day was a way to keep in touch with Black constituents, to hear their concerns, and to solicit votes. White politicians also sent letters of acknowledgement and messages to organizers in recognition of the special occasion. In 1935 Conservative prime minister Richard B. Bennett and Ontario premier Mitch Hepburn both sent official greetings to Walter Perry and the BAACB in Windsor. Some also issued official public announcements in support of the annual affair.

Canadians of European origin took part in August First street processions. All-White marching bands of fraternal orders and other community organizations participated in Emancipation Day parades. In 1896 two White women rode on one of the dozens of carriage floats in London that were filled with Black women and children. Some Whites also participated in cakewalk dance competitions, picnics, baseball games, races, and other leisure activities. White participation was occasionally limited because some Emancipation Day activities were restricted to

EMANCIPATION DAY	JOUR DE L'ÉMANCIPATION
August 25, 2006	**Le 25 août 2006**
WHEREAS, the City of Ottawa recognizes the diversity of its citizens; and	**ATTENDU QUE** la Ville d'Ottawa reconnaît la diversité de ses citoyens;
WHEREAS, the City of Ottawa acknowledges the historic significance of the 1793 Emancipation Act as the first Act against the institution of slavery in the British Empire and the precursor to the Emancipation Act of 1834; and	**ATTENDU QUE** la Ville d'Ottawa reconnaît l'importance historique de la *Loi sur l'émancipation* de 1793 comme première loi contre l'esclavage dans l'Empire britannique, précurseur de la *Loi sur l'émancipation* de 1834;
WHEREAS, the Emancipation Act, August 1, 1834 was intended to end slavery in the British Empire; and	**ATTENDU QUE** la *Loi sur l'émancipation* du 1er août 1834 avait pour objet de mettre fin à l'esclavage dans l'Empire britannique;
WHEREAS, August 1st is celebrated by the descendants of these enslaved persons as Emancipation Day;	**ATTENDU QUE** le 1er août est célébré comme étant le Jour de l'émancipation par les descendants des personnes réduites à l'esclavage;
THEREFORE, I, Bob Chiarelli, Mayor of the City of Ottawa do hereby proclaim **August 25, 2006 as Emancipation Day in the City of Ottawa**, a day of jubilation from tribulation in the City of Ottawa.	**PAR CONSÉQUENT,** je, Bob Chiarelli, maire d'Ottawa, proclame par la présente **le 25 août 2006 Jour de l'émancipation à Ottawa**, une journée de réjouissance de la fin des souffrances dans la Ville d'Ottawa.

Bob Chiarelli
Mayor / Maire

In 2006 the City of Ottawa issued its proclamation declaring August 1st Emancipation Day.

Courtesy of the City of Ottawa.

Blacks only. For example, when the cakewalk competition began at the gala in Hamilton in 1888, the chairman announced, "Ladies and gentlemen, the first quadrille will be danced exclusively by colored people. After that you may use your own judgement. The implied invitation was largely accepted later in the evening."[9]

After the abolition of American slavery in 1865, there was a decrease in White involvement, largely because many believed that the goals of Emancipation Day had been reached. Nonetheless, Whites continued to participate to some degree and were always welcome. During the early 1900s, Whites, for the most part, were observers. White speakers still gave addresses and Whites attended as family members of interracial marriages.

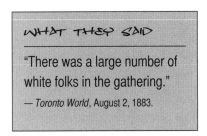

WHAT THEY SAID

"There was a large number of white folks in the gathering."
— *Toronto World*, August 2, 1883.

FIRST NATIONS

Blacks and Natives had sometimes contradictory relationships in early Canada. People of African descent were enslaved by Natives in Upper Canada, and Blacks first came to the Grand River reserve area in Brantford, Ontario, as slaves. Sophia Pooley, for example, was owned by Joseph Brant as a young girl. Natives also traded enslaved Africans between Canada and the United States. In more positive interactions, Aboriginals provided directions, food, clothing, money, and transportation to runaways like Josiah Henson and his family, who received assistance from Natives in Ohio on their way to Canada from Kentucky. In addition, Black and Native men fought together in the War of 1812 to defend British interests against the United States.

Mohawk Loyalists like Joseph Brant's three sons and other Iroquois militiamen received land grants at Grand River. Former slaves, including Black Loyalist Peter Long's son-in-law Aaron Eyres, who fought in the War of 1812, took refuge on the Grand River Reserve and received land plots from Joseph Brant. Fugitive slaves who immigrated in the late eighteenth century and throughout the nineteenth century were welcomed to settle on reserve land on the Six

Nations Reserve. African Canadians and Aboriginals lived among each other in Brantford, in Nova Scotia, and in other parts of Canada. They became family through marriage. In one such instance, Brant's daughter Elizabeth married an ex-slave named John Morey and lived in Brantford. Their daughter Catherine Morey married escaped slave John H. Henderson from Maryland and also lived in Brantford. In Nova Scotia, formerly enslaved Black men and Mi'kmaq women married.

Ethel Alexander (back, left) and Nina Mae Alexander (back, right), circa 1919. They taught at the No. 2 Six Nations School in Grand River south of Brantford, Ontario, between 1914 and 1920. Their brother Arthur Alexander taught at the No. 7 Six Nations School from 1916 to 1920.

Courtesy of the Spencer Alexander Collection.

Black teachers taught Six Nations children on the Grand River Reserve south of Brantford. Between 1914 and 1922, Nina Mae, Ethel Lanonia, and Arthur Alexander were employed by the Six Nations School Board. The Alexander family of Anderdon Township, near Amherstburg, contained a long line of educators. They were second generation descendants of an escaped slave. Their father, John Henry Alexander, was the principal of the King Street School in Amherstburg from 1880 to1917.

Natives and Blacks also shared similar social experiences in early Canada. Both First Nations people and individuals of African descent were enslaved by the French and British. The treatment that both groups endured was inhumane; although in different ways, African Canadians and Natives experienced racism and marginalization in mainstream Canadian society. In the 1950s through to the 1970s, both groups fought to bring public awareness to the human rights violations they faced, including discrimination in employment, education, and housing, as well as the problems of police violence and segregation. At times Blacks and Natives joined forces through social organizations to address systemic racism and push for anti-discrimination laws.

Blacks and Natives developed social relationships as neighbours, friends, family, activists, and colleagues. Therefore, it is not surprising that Natives participated in Emancipation Day commemorations. Native brass bands, such as the 37th Haldimand Rifles, the Grand River Indian Brass Band, the Osheweken Indian Cornet Band, the Victoria Brass Band of the Six Nations, and the Muncey Indian Band, marched in parades in Woodstock, Brantford, Hamilton, and London. The earliest known recorded Emancipation Day celebration in Brantford was on August 1, 1856, and took place at a grove on the site of the Mohawk Institute on the Six Nations Reserve, the current location of the Woodland Cultural Centre. It is likely that First Nations people would have also taken part in other aspects of the yearly observance, as it would have been an extension of their similarly oppressed history and their pursuit of liberty.

The 37th Haldimand Rifles Brass Band taken at the Niagara Camp, Niagara-on-the-Lake, June 1910. They were members of a regiment of active Six Nations militia men that was originally formed in 1866 to protect Upper Canada from Fenian attacks. Many of the men enlisted to fight in the First World War.

Courtesy of the Woodland Cultural Centre.

AMERICAN VISITORS

African-American visitors came from neighbouring American cities to celebrate Emancipation Day. They travelled from places in Michigan such as Detroit, Flint, and Ann Arbor, from Cincinnati, Ohio, and from cities in New York State such as Buffalo, Utica, and Rochester. They also came from Cleveland, Ohio; Gary, Indiana; and from as far as Louisville, Kentucky; Chicago, Illinois; Boston, Massachusetts; as well as Georgia and Alabama. The Blacks visiting from the United States visited relatives who lived in Canada, owned summer cottages in places like Shrewsbury on the shore of Lake Erie southeast of Buxton, or were Black civil rights activists.

Before 1865 these visitors joined in celebrating the freedom that was denied to their fellow enslaved Americans and to use British abolition as a catalyst to push for American liberation. African-American abolitionists such as Frederick Douglass, William Howard Day, and William J. Watkins were invited to speak at anniversaries across Ontario. After 1865 they participated in the dual emancipation celebrations that included Lincoln Day.

Invited to address Canadians celebrating Emancipation Day were a mixture of American speakers, including White American clergymen, like Samuel Joseph May from Boston, Massachusetts, who spoke in Windsor in 1852; Black lawyer Orra L. C. Hughes, from Pennsylvania, who was the keynote speaker in 1878 in Hamilton; and African-American lawyer and Illinois Republican representative Edward H. Morris of Chicago, who addressed the audience in Hamilton in 1884.

In the 1950s and 1960s, Black civil rights activists were invited to deliver speeches to Emancipation Day crowds in Canada. Adam Clayton Powell Jr., Martin Luther King Jr., Daisy Bates, Reverend Fred Shuttlesworth, and Mrs. Medgar "Myrlie" Evers are just a handful of the honoured guest speakers. August First in Canada was a demonstration of North American unity for the cause of human rights.

This very diverse group of celebrants participated in the traditional aspects of Emancipation Day commemorations for various reasons: remembrance of their ancestors, promoting self-identity and human rights, and preserving local, Canadian, and international Black history and culture.

CHAPTER FIVE.

CHURCH SERVICES: FREEDOM, FAITH, AND FELLOWSHIP

"Oh freedom! Oh freedom! Oh freedom over me. And before I'd be a slave, I'll be buried in my grave, and go home to my Lord and be free."
— *OH FREEDOM*, NEGRO SPIRITUAL.

Attending church thanksgiving services were an important part of Emancipation Day observances. People attended the church of their choice — whether the African or British Methodist Episcopal, or a Baptist, Anglican, or Wesleyan denomination — to give God thanks for delivering them, their relatives, and their ancestors from slavery and to express gratitude for the legal acknowledgement of their God-given rights. Many African Canadians held strong Christian beliefs and connected their flight from slavery in North America and the Caribbean to the Biblical experience of the Hebrews who were delivered out of bondage in Egypt. African Americans who escaped slavery considered themselves to be a chosen people, handpicked by God to make the pilgrimage to Canada, which they called Canaan, the land of milk and honey promised by God to his children. Blacks had remained faithful that God would put an end to the evil of slavery, and when they were brought out of captivity with the passage of the Slavery Abolition Act of 1833, the long-awaited day had to be rejoiced.

Churches were also important in meeting the needs of Black communities. They were not only places of worship, but also served as early schools for those Black children not permitted to attend local public schools in many towns and cities in Ontario, Nova Scotia, New Brunswick, and Alberta. Local public school boards in areas of these provinces did not want Black children attending school with White children and legally established separate schools based on race. Sometimes, even though Black parents paid taxes to support local schools like White parents, there were no school facilities for them, or if there was, the conditions were very poor. Therefore, community churches provided education programs to serve the needs of children and adult learners, ensuring future success for students and the African-Canadian community as a whole.

Churches also functioned as charity organizations for arriving fugitive slaves in need of food, clothing, and shelter, and as social centres where parties, concerts, banquets, and other celebrations were held. Additionally, churches were meeting places for various political gatherings, like anti-slavery meetings.

Church ministers were revered leaders and educators of the community. Therefore, it was not surprising that Black churches were established in Canada as soon as a small community assembled. The earliest Black congregation, Toronto's First Baptist Church, started in 1827. Other early ones include the Nazrey AME Church in Amherstburg that was established in 1848. The Baptist church in Halifax, now called the Cornwallis Street Baptist Church, was founded in 1832. The BME Church in St. Catharines, Salem Chapel, opened in 1820 and moved to a larger building in 1855 to accommodate a growing congregation. While she lived in St. Catharines, Harriet Tubman was one of its worshippers. The Beth Emmanuel BME Church in London (also called Fugitive Slave Chapel) was established in 1848. Present-day Stewart Memorial Church in Hamilton was originally St. Paul's AME Church, which was started in 1835. Turner AME Church in Oakville was established in 1891. Brantford's AME and BME churches also opened in the mid-1830s. Several of these churches remain open and active today.

White churches also started missions to aid fugitive slaves coming in to Canada from the American South. For instance, mission schools were organized to educate young and adult students in London, Amherstburg, Hamilton, Queen's Bush, Dresden, Chatham, and Buxton. Special August First church services were led by church preachers, both Black and White, and it was very common for these churches to sponsor Emancipation Day events.

Services were traditionally held on the Sunday morning or evening of the three-day weekend celebration, and usually Sundays were devoted to spiritual activities and upliftment through religious speeches.

In 1854 a sunrise service was held in Toronto. People assembled at 5:00 a.m. at the Second Wesleyan Chapel on Richmond Street to "offer up devout thanksgiving to Almighty God for His past mercies, and to engage in fervent prayer for the utter extinction of Slavery and other parts of the world where the evil now exists."[1] For the fifth anniversary of August First in Toronto, a church service was held at the AME church, which at that time was located at Richmond and York streets. The sermon, based on scriptures from the Bible, was delivered by Reverend William Miller, a free Black man and anti-slavery activist from Philadelphia. As part of his sermon, Miller offered special prayers on behalf of Queen Victoria, her family, and her nation.

Robert Gordon, a Black Jamaican clergyman, delivered a sermon in 1859 in London, Canada West (Ontario), in St. Paul's Anglican Cathedral. The church, in partnership with the Colonial Church and School Society, established a fugitive slave mission in 1854 called the Free Coloured Mission. It served the religious, educational and social needs of incoming refugees from the United States. Gordon's August First audience included many of London's Blacks and African-Canadian visitors from other areas of the province. He started his religious lecture by noting the importance of celebration:

This is the cover of the sermon delivered by the Reverend Robert Gordon on August 1, 1859. A Sermon on the Morning of the 1st of August 1859, by a Black Clergyman, the Reverend Robert Gordon, in St. Paul's Cathedral. London, Canada West, on the Occasion of the Celebration of the Twenty-First Anniversary of West Indian Emancipation, by the Colored Citizens of London, and Several other Places. *London, Ontario: Colonial Church and School Society, Mission to the Fugitive Slaves in Canada, 1859.* While in London, Ontario, in 1858 and 1859, Robert taught weekly Bible classes, conducted daily visits to the homes of fugitives, and assisted Reverend Thomas Hughes in teaching Black and White students at the Colonial Church and School Society mission school.

A SERMON

PREACHED ON THE MORNING OF THE FIRST OF
AUGUST, 1859,

BY A BLACK CLERGYMAN,

THE REV. ROBERT GORDON,

IN

ST. PAUL'S CATHEDRAL,

LONDON, CANADA WEST,

ON THE OCCASION OF THE CELEBRATION OF THE
TWENTY-FIRST ANNIVERSARY OF

WEST INDIAN EMANCIPATION,

BY THE COLORED CITIZENS OF LONDON, AND
SEVERAL OTHER PLACES.

LONDON, C. W.
PRINTED AT THE OFFICE OF THE DAILY PROTOTYPE, RICHMOND STREET.

1859.

It well becomes the colored people to consider this day as a Festival; since, enjoying here, as they can do wherever the British Banner is unfurled, as indicative of territorial possession, the blessed privilege of sitting unmolested under their own vine and fig tree, protected as well as their white brethren by laws which are impartially administered, they cannot but cordially sympathise with those who, prior to the 1st day of August, 1838, had not been possessors of such invaluable benefits. [2]

During this period, the symbolism of the British flag for Blacks changed from representing bondage and oppression to standing for freedom and protection. Gordon went on to discuss the significance of August 1, 1838, when the apprentice system ended early in Barbados, Jamaica, Guyana, and South Africa, giving complete freedom to all Blacks:

On the morning of the 1st of August 1838, he [slaves] entered into the full enjoyment of his rights, and was no longer either a slave, or a half freeman, but was, to all intents and purposes, as free as those devoted and philanthropic friends of the outcasts by whose unceasing efforts his birthright was *restored* to him.[3]

He blessed the day's remaining programme and instructed listeners, "Joyfully celebrate the Jubilee of the West Indian Emancipation, and enter with cheerfulness, decorum, and propriety, into those festivities which your exertions have provided."[4] By the end of that week, Gordon printed and sold copies of his sermons to benefit the efforts of the London mission.

As an extension of their diverse role in the Black community, churches regularly hosted August First gatherings:

Robert Gordon was born in Jamaica in 1836. While attending school as a teenager, he became involved in the Church of England, even though his parents were members of the Methodist faith. He faced racial discrimination in his attempts to become an ordained priest of the church in Jamaica and left for England in search of more promising opportunities. Gordon was appointed to the Colonial Church and School Society, the mission arm of the church, and accepted a post in London, Ontario, to work with fugitives from slavery in the fall of 1858. While there, the bishop of Huron, Benjamin Cronyn, ordained Gordon as a deacon and later a priest. Gordon was put in charge of the fugitive slave mission. He returned to Jamaica in 1861 for six years and was appointed the headmaster, or principal, of Wolmer's Grammar School in Kingston, where he worked until 1867, when he left again for England. There, he preached at several churches and published a book, *The Jamaican Church: Why it Failed*, that spoke out against the existence of racism and colonialism in Jamaica's Anglican Church. He died in England of pneumonia in 1885.

... A. M. E. Church, in the province of Canada, will hereafter celebrate the first of August, that memorable day when eight hundred thousand of our oppressed brethren were emancipated by the British Government. By opening our chapels for divine service, and in invoking the blessing of the Almighty God, upon her Majesty the Queen, and country.[5]

This declaration showed church leaders' determination to keep Emancipation Day commemorations grounded in God so that the importance of prayer and thanksgiving would never be forgotten. It also reinforced the position of the Black church at the centre of the community.

For at least twenty years, White church minister Henry James Grasett of St. James' Anglican Cathedral in Toronto was involved in Emancipation Day commemorations. He delivered sermons at the church and nearby St. Lawrence Hall in Toronto between 1839 and 1856. Henry went through "the usual and beautiful exercise of prayer, peculiar to the Episcopal church, he delivered an eloquent discourse of British West Indies Emancipation."[6] In 1840, celebrants paraded to St. James for religious services conducted by Archdeacon Grasett. Newspaper articles show that he also led services in 1854, 1856, and 1860. Based on his longstanding participation in an event related to eradicating slavery, it can be concluded that Reverend Grasett was a committed abolitionist. As such, it is certain that Grasett would have spoken out against American slavery, encouraged gatherers to continue to agitate for its end, and emphasized the importance of a strong, cohesive society.

At St. Thomas Anglican Church in Hamilton on the August 1, 1864, Reverend Charles Henry Drinkwater, a man of European descent, conducted an Emancipation Day church service that focused on obtaining freedom through faith in God. His lengthy sermon, along with the proceedings of the special day, were published in a small book and sold for five cents a copy.

Church pastors at this time also played the role of teacher, because many members of their congregations in the early 1800s could not read or write if they were fugitive slaves, or if they had worked and not attended school when they were young. For ministers that were activists, Emancipation Day sermons focused mainly on freedom, faith, and taught about the atrocities of slavery. They also discussed how to approach the future and how to take advantage of the opportunities available in the free North.

Evening thanksgiving services were also held regularly. In 1857 William Howard Day, an African-American abolitionist who was born free in New York and had lived in Buxton for a short while (1856–1859), delivered a well-received key speech at the First Baptist Church in Chatham. An evening service was hosted by the Young Men's Christian Association at Bonaventure Hall in Montreal in 1861. The program opened with the singing of hymns, followed by prayers and

William Howard Day had visited Canada West regularly from 1843 until he decided to live there in the 1850s. He came to assist freedom seekers who emigrated to Canada. Day taught at schools that were established to provide an education for former African American slaves. He also worked in various jobs in order to raise money to provide financial help to fugitives in need. Day also lived in Hamilton and St. Catharines, which were other communities with high populations of fugitive slaves. He became involved in John Brown's planning of the 1859 Harpers Ferry attack, printing John Brown's *Provisional Constitution* at an unknown location in St. Catharines. Day left for England in 1859 for a speaking tour and then returned to the United States.

speeches about the benefits of British citizenship and the anticipation that the end of the Civil War would mean freedom of their African-American brothers and sisters. The American Civil War (1861–1865) began when eleven slaveholding states in the South declared that they wanted to withdraw from the United States and form their own confederacy to preserve the practice of slavery. The Union, made up of free Northern States, wanted to keep the country together and abolish slavery in the South.[7]

The songs sung in church, called hymnals and spirituals, were a soulful expression of gratitude to God for freeing them and their ancestors from bondage and the determination of African Canadians to persevere against tremendous odds with God's grace. Songs like "Swing Low, Sweet Chariot," "Wherever He Leads, I'll Go," "He Leadeth Me," "I'm Free Praise the Lord I'm Free," "What a Friend We Have in Jesus," and "We Shall Overcome" were a few of the favourite songs that conveyed these messages.

Church-sponsored Emancipation Day functions were not just limited to serious religious activities. It was one of few occasions when African Canadians gathered in large numbers to honour their heroes and display racial pride. During the 1800s through to the early 1900s, social activities revolved around the church. Also during this era, Blacks were not welcome to participate in mainstream social activities, or if they were, faced separation because of their race. Therefore, Black churches organized all kinds of events to meet the social needs of the community, especially as part of big celebrations like Emancipation Day, including picnics, parties with various kinds of "respectable" entertainment, and musical concerts with performances by gospel choirs. The women of the church cooked sumptuous feasts for many of these events. In 1929 Reverend C.E. Perry and the Oakville AME church hosted a garden party at Victoria Park, at Lakeshore Road West and Chalmers Street. Christian beliefs and practices, which regulated the lives of many African Canadians, were elaborately intertwined into Emancipation Day festivities.

Reverend Walter Hawkins was the Bishop of the BME Church, Canada Conference, from 1886 until his death in 1894. He was the pastor of the BME Church, Victoria Chapel, in Chatham. As a prominent leader in the Black community, Hawkins delivered speeches at Emancipation Day commemorations, like in 1871 in his home town of Chatham.

Courtesy of the Chatham-Kent Museum, 1985-27-2-72.

CHAPTER SIX

THE PARADE:
MARCHING TOWARD FREEDOM

We're marching on to freedom land, we're marching on to freedom land.
God's our strength from day to day, as we walk the narrow way.
We're going forward, we're going forward.
One day we're going to be free.
— "We're Marching on to Freedom Land," Carlton Reese,
Voices of the Civil Rights Movement: Black American Freedom Songs
1960–1966, Smithsonian Folkways, 1997.

The parade was the main attraction of most Emancipation Day celebrations. Parades were very popular in North American cities during the 1800s and 1900s and remains so today. For Emancipation Day, street processions became a significant feature of the annual tradition to commemorate the end of the enslavement of Africans, to mark the anniversary of the abolition of slavery, and to celebrate freedom. What made the parades so appealing, drawing hundreds and even thousands of people annually? How were they organized and structured to appeal to the masses year after year? What did the crowds see and hear?

SPOTLIGHT ON ...

James Lewis, like Ray's great-grandparents on his father's side and grandparents on his mother's side, was a former slave who escaped to Canada. He operated a business as a barber and hairdresser in Simcoe, Ontario. Ray Lewis was born in Hamilton in 1910, and in the 1932 summer Olympics he became the first African-Canadian athlete to win an Olympic medal for the 4 x 100 relay. Ray Lewis was a special guest at Emancipation Day in Windsor in the 1930s. In honour of his achievements and his ability to overcome racial discrimination, Ray was awarded the Order of Canada in 2001. A Hamilton school was named after him in 2005, and in 2010 he was inducted into the Hamilton Sports Hall of Fame.

Raymond Gray Lewis often ran alongside railway tracks to practise for track and field while he worked as a porter. He was given the nickname "Rapid Ray" because of his ability to run fast.

Courtesy of the Hamilton Spectator.

PARADE MARSHALS

The ceremonial title of grand marshal was given to a special guest or dignitary, often a recognized community leader, and this person was chosen to lead the parade. In the nineteenth century, grand marshals, mounted on horses, led the parade of marchers, carriages, and floats. They were also the official greeters for those arriving from out of town by steamer or train and were responsible for ensuring an orderly public demonstration.

Moses Brantford Jr. was appointed the grand marshal for the parade in Amherstburg in 1894, as shown in the image on the cover of this book. James Lewis, the maternal grandfather of Hamilton-born track athlete and railway porter Ray Lewis, was chosen to be the grand marshal three times: 1884, 1888, and 1893, all of these in Hamilton.

Mounted assistant marshals helped to guide the procession and ensure it ran smoothly, directing the line of the march as it wound its way through the main streets. Charles Peyton Lucas, a blacksmith and a former slave from Virginia, was the assistant marshal of the 1854 August First parade in Toronto. Later on in the twentieth century, with the introduction of the automobile, parade marshals led marchers in decorated convertibles. As another example, Windsor's 1954 parade was marshalled by a seven-man motorcycle squad.

SPOTLIGHT ON ...

Charles Peyton Lucas was a self-emancipated man from Virginia. He ran away in 1841 in his early twenties and eventually settled in Toronto by 1852, after making his way north to protect his family from the 1850 Fugitive Slave Law. As a teenager, Charles was hired out as an apprentice to a blacksmith and trained in that skilled trade. He went on to become a blacksmith in Toronto and was noted as an exceptional shoer of horses. Charles, his wife Catherine, and their three children lived on Centre Street in downtown Toronto, near Osgoode Hall, which had a large population of fugitive slaves. His children attended the neighbourhood school. Always a very active supporter of the Black community, he was a marshal in an Emancipation Day parade in Elmira, New York, in 1850. Charles died in Toronto in January 1870 at the age of fifty.

MARCHING BANDS

A uniformed musical band followed the Grand Marshal in the procession. Hired bands provided lively entertainment with their horns, drums, cornets, trombones, clarinets, violins, guitars, and banjos. Most of these regimental marching bands were made up of volunteer militiamen and war veterans. The former soldiers who played in August First parades were exceptionally artistic because it was common for Black men to be the musicians in most military units.

Military bands regulated everyday life for soldiers in service. They gave signals or provided coded orders during battle, lifted the spirits of soldiers during wartime, and performed tattoos — outdoor military exercises that were evening entertainment for

Celebrants packed the grandstand at Jackson Park to watch the spectacular parade enter the grounds.

Courtesy of the E. Andrea Shreve Moore Collection, Essex County Black Historical Research Society.

troops. The Weaver Band from Chatham, named after politician and business owner Henry Weaver, was led by drum major John Freeman at Windsor's 1895 parade. The Excelsior Band of Chatham, under captain and drum major Jack Richards, was one of the marching bands in the 1883 Toronto procession, and the Sons of Union from Detroit were invited to march in the parade in Windsor in 1852.

The tunes played by the bands were a musical expression of Blacks' heartfelt loyalty to Britain and the ideas of national and cultural identity they held. Bands played patriotic pieces such as "God Save the Queen," "The Star Spangled Banner," and later "O Canada." They also played popular folk songs and good-time music like "When the Saints Go Marching In," anti-slavery songs like "Get off the Track," and marching songs like "John Brown's Body." There were woodwind, string, brass, or fife and drum bands. Parade-goers listened to the Harrow Brass Band of Essex County play in Amherstburg in 1894 and the Union Brass Band from Hamilton in Chatham in 1874. Scott's Cornet Band and Reed Brass Band from Buffalo played in Brantford in 1894 and Cleveland's Drum and Bugle Corps marched in 1970 in Windsor.

Along with regimental bands, other musical ensembles that marched in Emancipation Day processions during the nineteenth and twentieth centuries included police bands, community band groups, professional troupes, concert bands, and drill teams from Ontario and the United States. John W. "Jack" Johnson was an exceptionally talented bandleader. The London, Ontario, native moved to Michigan and founded the Detroit City Band in the early 1880s. He returned to his hometown to lead the Forest City Band at the end of that decade. Local musical bands such as the Windsor City Band, the Optimists Youth Band, and the South Windsor Lions were also regular players.

SPOTLIGHT ON ...

Henry Weaver escaped slavery in America and settled in Chatham with his wife, Annie. They purchased a building, where Henry owned and operated a butcher shop downstairs, while his wife ran a small inn upstairs. She rented rooms to Black travellers who were denied accommodations at local White-owned hotels because of their race. Henry was the first Black man elected as a city councillor in Chatham, serving from 1891 to 1893 and again from 1895 to 1898. He was also very involved in the Black Masonic lodges of the city. The Weaver Band was named in recognition of his community achievements and his personal support for the band.

The Weeks Band from
Thorold (near Niagara Falls),
the Chatham City Band, the
Eureka Colored Band from
Niagara, the Forest City
Band of London, the Detroit
City Band, and the Mount
Pavement Band from Detroit
were just a few of the hun-
dreds of bands that performed
in Emancipation Day parades
across Ontario in the 1800s.

The North Buxton Maple Leaf Marching Band. Ira. T Shadd offered music classes to families in North Buxton and once the student's skills developed, they became members of the band.

Courtesy of the Buxton National Historic Site & Museum.

The well-known North Buxton Maple Leaf Band was formed by Ira T. Shadd in 1955. They participated in Emancipation Day parades in Windsor, beginning in 1956 and regularly after that. Historian, author, and researcher Adrienne Shadd was a majorette in the North Buxton Maple Leaf Band in the 1960s. She recalls that their most notable marching song was "The Maple Leaf Forever," recently revived by Michael Bublé at the closing ceremonies of the 2010 Winter Olympics, in Vancouver.

African-American drill bands performed elaborate manoeuvres based on military drills as part of Windsor's parade. One such group was the popular French Dukes Precision Drill Team from Ann Arbor, Michigan, who performed annually between 1966 and 1970. People who attended Emancipation Day celebrations in Windsor as a child during the 1950s and 1960s identify the drill teams as their most memorable recollection. One person states, "The drill units were replete in military uniform and toting rifles. Their drills and routines were so rhythmic and exact."[1] Another individual recalls, "I especially remember the military style bands with the young men and women performing the most exquisite precision drill marches. The French Dukes from Michigan were my favourite. They routinely won the Emancipation Day contest for the best drill team."[2]

Walter Perry, organizer of Windsor's Greatest Freedom Show on Earth, scouted and invited talented Ohio, Michigan, and Indiana singers and bands to participate in Emancipation Day festivities. The talents of drill teams and baton twirlers were showcased when they marched. Majorettes, which were young female dancers, accompanied marching bands beginning in the mid-1950s. The majorettes twirled batons skilfully while performing choreographed movements.

The French Dukes Precision Drill Team were regular winners for the best drill team at Emancipation Day celebrations in Windsor during the 1960s, due to their exceptional talent. Formed in 1962, the group went on to win every state and national competition they entered.

From the *Ann Arbor News*, September 8, 1968. Courtesy of the Herald Company, Inc.

Strike up the band!

Everyone loves a parade. One of the highlights of Emancipation Day celebrations for many years, has been the colorful parade which has officially opened the event. Leading units of both races have been proud to participate. The throngs of people which have jammed the route of march, testify to the fact that this is, in fact, Windsor's brightest, most anticipated, annual parade. A few scenes from previous years are shown here.

Several snapshots of Windsor's Emancipation Day parade in 1947 that highlight the diversity of the marching bands.

Courtesy of the E. Andrea Shreve Moore Collection, Essex County Black Historical Research Society.

A variety of other ethnic marching bands participated in the August First parades. Several First Nations and European bands have performed throughout the celebration's history. Aboriginal bands included the Grand River Band, which performed in 1875 in Brantford. The 37th Haldimand Rifles, a regimental marching band made up of former soldiers from the Six Nations Reserve, played in Woodstock in 1898 and in Brantford in 1912. The Oshweken Indian Cornet Band marched in Hamilton's 1893 parade, and the Muncey (also spelled Munsee) Indian Band took part in Emancipation Day commemorations in London in 1895. White bands included the Toronto Victoria Band of the Orange Order, a fraternal organization of Protestant men of Scottish or North Irish heritage. They marched in St. Catharines in 1891 and in Brantford in 1903.

African Canadian and Native bands were also invited to play in other civic parades, including Victoria Day, Dominion Day, and Labour Day parades. They performed at public events that celebrated the British monarchy, such as royal visits and Queen Victoria's Golden and Diamond Jubilees in 1887 and 1897. These bands often played at agricultural shows across the province, and these performances were huge social events. The Canadian National Exhibition (CNE) was an agricultural show that featured farm animals, equipment, and recreational activities. They provided musical entertainment at political dinners, public anniversaries, opening ceremonies, and other public observations. Black and Native bands would take part in funeral processions for community leaders and elected officials. These bands also held annual tattoos that were widely attended.

Emancipation Day was definitely a multicultural affair. Although the majority of participants were of African heritage, people of different races not only marched alongside one another, but also interacted at various junctures of this huge exhibition.

SPOTLIGHT ON ...

The French Dukes Precision Drill Team was sponsored by the junior auxiliary of the Elks-Pratt Lodge No. 322, Improved Benevolent and Protective Order of the Elks of the World. The twenty-five Black youth, ages fifteen to eighteen, were selected to march in the 1969 inaugural parade for Richard Nixon in Washington, D.C.

MARCHERS

Marchers in August First parades represented various social and community organizations. Following behind the bands and veteran military units were numerous chapters of Black Masonic lodges: Prince Hall Grand Lodge of the Province of Ontario, the Grand United Order of Odd Fellows, and the Knights of Pythias. These fraternal orders were also involved in the organization of Emancipation Day celebrations, including St. John Lodge No. 9 of Chatham, Eureka Lodge No. 20 of Toronto, and Victoria Lodge No. 2 in St. Catharines, along with the groups mentioned in Chapter 3. The lodge's lady auxiliary groups were made up of the wives and daughters of male members. They sponsored carriages and cars in August First processions. The Women of the Order the Eastern Star, the Household of Ruth, the Daughters of Samaria, and the Star of Calanthe are some of the longstanding African-Canadian female organizations that were active in the community.

Literary groups, cultural clubs, benevolent societies, political groups, music and dance ensembles, school children, and African-Canadian temperance societies also marched in the parade. During the 1860s, there was a growing movement with settlers of both races to abstain from drinking alcohol, because they believed that it led to the ruin of individuals and society. The Temperance Society of Amherstburg and the Sons of Temperance in Hamilton were part of the trend to reduce the harmful impact of alcohol on the Black community.

One approach to improving the conditions of the community was to establish educational support groups such as the Chatham Literary and Debating Society and the Hour-A-Day Study Club in Windsor. The Chatham Literary and Debating Society, also called the Chatham Lyceum, was formed in 1872 by grocer Ezekiel C. Cooper and other board members to offer lectures and debates. Beginning in 1934, the women of the Hour-A-Day Study Club in Windsor dedicated sixty-minutes a day — hence the name — to expanding their intellect. They also encouraged childhood literacy by giving books to mothers with babies.

Associations that provided help to incoming fugitives included the Provincial Union Association, the Victorian Reform Benevolent Society, and various abolitionist societies in Ontario and Nova Scotia. As refugees from American slavery were a major concern during the mid-1800s, a considerable number of support groups arose. The Brotherly Union Society in Hamilton was a benevolent society. It was formed in 1862 by several community leaders to provide financial assistance to those in need. The Ladies Auxiliary of the Brotherhood of Sleeping Car Porters, Pullman Division, focused on educational programs and scholarships for young people from the 1940s through to 1957. Many organizations had a number of chapters across the province or the country, like the Universal Negro Improvement Association in Toronto, Montreal, and Nova Scotia (in Sydney, Halifax, and Glace Bay). African Canadians were frequently members of more than one organization. Community organizations had a strong presence in Emancipation Day parades.

WORDPLAY

A *benevolent society* is a voluntary organization that is established for the purpose of charity. They plan activities and events to raise money for a particular cause.

Male and female marchers dressed up in coloured costumes, elaborate dress, and full regalia or uniforms. Former soldiers wore their uniforms with pride while Black Masons donned their ceremonial dress. This was often vividly described in newspapers covering the events. One such account notes, "In line were the colored Knights Templars, in plumed helmets and drawn swords...."[3] Another describes a group of six Black freemasons masons "... dressed in gowns like a beadle's, three-cornered cocked hats with feathers, and white pants (excepting one carrying a sword whose costume was partly scarlet)."[4] When the female members of the Household of Ruth performed drills in Hamilton in 1884, they were described as looking stunning in their "regalia of gold braid and black velvet, with tiaras and crowns of glittering tinsel."[5]

Emancipation Celebration

JACKSON PARK, WINDSOR ONTARIO

Tues. Aug. 1st 1939

ENTERTAINMENT FOR EVERYBODY

Prominent Speakers from Canada and U.S.A.
Spiritual Program includes Speakers and
Singers of Radio Fame

➤ Free   Free **◄**

ICE CREAM & POP FOR CHILDREN

Arrangements has been made to take care of **2500** children

Childrens Program starts 1.30 to 4.30
Main Program Starts 4.30 to 8.30

**Races - Games - Vaudeville - Eats - Bar-B-Que
Kiddy Rides-Ferris Wheel - Many slaves to be present
Dancing - Open Air Pavillion to Isaac Goodwin**

Various Church Organizations will supply the food

Everybody welcome renew old acquaintances and make new friends

Seating Capacity 10,000 Finest Park in Canada

Make this a Home Coming

*A poster advertising the 1939
Emancipation Day festivities in
Windsor.*

**Courtesy of the E. Andrea Shreve
Moore Collection, Essex County
Black Historical Research Society.**

PARADE SYMBOLS

Many symbols have been part of August First parades. Participants proudly waved flags: the Union Jack, the Stars and Stripes of the United States, and later the Canadian flag. Most people carried banners and signs with political and anti-slavery messages, such as "God, humanity, the Queen, and a free country," "Sons of England," and "Am I not a man and a brother?" which means that God made all men from one blood. Banners and sashes identified the assorted groups of marchers as they passed. The emblems of Black Masonic orders and other participating organizations were displayed with confidence, and other symbols representing Britain and America, such as John Bull and Uncle Sam — the respective icons of each country's patriotism — were much in evidence.

Freedom, history, and remembrance have been regular themes since 1834. Pamphlets, flyers, leaflets, and posters were distributed or posted along parade routes to encourage people to participate in community initiatives that addressed specific issues of concern to African Canadians once Emancipation Day celebrations were over, issues such as the abolition of American slavery, segregated schools in Ontario, Nova Scotia, and New Brunswick, or the other numerous concerns during the Civil Rights Era. In 1964 Toronto marchers carried a placard with the words "Canada needs racial equality, too!"

Programme booklets were another form of text used to communicate with Emancipation Day visitors. They were distributed or sold at various Emancipation Day venues, local businesses, and community organizations. First published in Windsor in 1948, the Emancipation Day event magazine *Progress: An Official Record of the Achievements of the Coloured Race*, printed annual issues that contained articles and interviews highlighting the achievements of people of African descent, photos and images of Blacks, advertisements for Black and White owned businesses, and the weekend programme of Emancipation Day events.

James Mink earned his riches by operating Toronto's largest livery stable, on Adelaide Street, and a hotel called the Mansion Inn, at the corner of Richmond and York streets. James and his brother George (the sons of freedom seekers) owned stage coach companies that transported mail and federal prisoners between Toronto and Kingston. James also provided his service to the mayor and city councillors of Toronto.

In an unfortunate turn of events, James gave his daughter's hand in marriage to a White man who was from Yorkshire in northern England, who then took her to the United States under the guise of going on a honeymoon and sold her into slavery. It took James large amounts of time and money to purchase his daughter's freedom and bring her back to Canada.

PARADE FLOATS

August First street processions included very popular float entries that honoured the occasion. Horse-drawn carriages, wagons, and later automobiles well-decorated with streamers, ribbons, flags, and flowers were pulled or driven through the main streets: "One feature of the morning procession was quite impressive — that of a car, beautifully decorated with flowers, etc., forming a canopy, under which were seated, we should judge, at least thirty little girls tastefully arrayed in white, and with wreaths of flowers on their heads."[6] In London in 1896, seventeen out of twenty carriages carried women, two of them were White.

It would take days, weeks, or even months to design, create, and build floats. Throughout the year, fundraisers were held and time, money, and materials were donated to make marvellous floats. They were used to communicate various messages such as the death of slavery. Different effigies, which are crafted representations of a disliked person or political idea, which represented slavery, were included in parades, and their destruction symbolized the abolition of slavery. In Hamilton in 1859, men of the Masonic lodge Sons of Uriah carried axes as a symbol of the downfall of the slave master. Floats also depicted topics of historical significance and promoted pride. Carriages and convertible cars carried dignitaries, community leaders, and guests of honour. Open-back trucks were used to transport children in the parade. Motorcades, a procession of vehicles, were another prominent aspect of the parade.

Emancipation Day parades often left a lasting mark on the viewer. In the 1850s, the daughter of Canadian author Susannah Moodie, Agnes Chamberlin, who was then in her early twenties,

THE PARADE: MARCHING TOWARD FREEDOM

recalled seeing James Mink, one of the wealthiest Black people in Toronto, in the first carriage of the parade, being drawn by eight horses.

THE SPECTATORS

Parades were an opportunity to make a grand public show. The amount of observers lining the parade routes ranged from dozens to hundreds, sometimes as many as ten deep. People also watched parades from rooftops and second- and third-story windows. The large audiences included spectators from near and far, from all kinds of backgrounds.

Spectators were given a visual treat. Gestures and shouts were exchanged as the procession passed, and goodies were thrown to the crowds. The role of the parade observer was important — certainly the demonstration was put on to entertain them, but the parade also served to educate them for a lifetime and to motivate them to take action in their communities in the days that would follow.

To ensure a good turnout, the public had to be informed of the parade well in advance. Emancipation Day committees placed ads in local newspapers and distributed flyers weeks before the actual events. One reason for this was to ensure that Black workers could get the day off if August First fell on a weekday. In one instance, the African Abolition Society, which

CELEBRATION

THE Abolition Society intend to celebrate the Anniversary of the Abolition of Slavery in the British Dominions, on the First of August next, by a PICNIC, &c., to take place at Belmont. The Committee of Management therefore request the attendance of all the colored people of Halifax and the vicinity, and all the Friends of Liberty and Freedom. They would likewise appeal to the Ladies and Gentlemen of Halifax for permission to the colored servants in their employ, to hold this one day of rejoicing as a holiday.

A procession will start at 9 o'clock from the African School House, and proceed to Church, where service will commence at 10 o'clock, after which they will proceed to Belmont, and pass the remainder of the day in healthful and innocent enjoyments. Tickets to be obtained at the gate. Entrance 77. By order of the President.

THOMAS JONHNSON.
July 17.   Secretary.

— *British Colonist* (Halifax), July 19, 1851

was sponsoring Emancipation Day in Halifax in 1851, requested — right in their advertisement — that White employers give their Black employees the day off.

Parades varied in scale and duration, from small processions that lasted for a brief time to massive demonstrations that lasted for two hours. Emancipation Day processions were a public occasion filled with pomp, ceremony, pageantry, and carnival motifs. It was a visual experience, and generally the most anticipated event of Emancipation Day.

Together, the various elements of the parades told stories of resistance, victory, freedom, and achievement, as well as the importance of memorializing African ancestors, Black history, and African-Canadian customs. The parade also served as a way to interact with the larger Black community and mainstream society. It reflected the structure of the local Black community and mirrored the values community members held, such as equality and justice. The organizers, marchers, and many of the people that watched the affair were the ones who assisted and contributed to the development of the Black community. The yearly public demonstration was also about making a political statement on issues of concern, such as racial discrimination in employment, housing, public businesses, and the presence of segregated schools, but it also served to mobilize community members around these matters. The other important point made by processions was that African Canadians were capable of conducting themselves in an orderly, well-behaved, and civilized fashion, debunking many myths and stereotypes. Some blatant misconceptions about Blacks existed into the twentieth century: that they were lazy, uncivilized, rowdy, and ill-mannered.

August First parades were also a public display of Black solidarity, strengthened with the inclusion of multiple generations. Additionally, the marches were a place to publically challenge the White dominance of the other days of the year. Purposely, Blacks occupied the most prominent streets of the town or city, areas that in some cases would otherwise not be accessible to them because of their race. Lastly, the processions symbolized racial pride.

CARIBANA

Caribana, the Trinidadian-style carnival parade, has roots in Emancipation Day commemorations in the West Indies. Since 1967, the vibrant festival has attracted spectators of all cultural backgrounds, with a large number of them being African Americans who go to Toronto to "jump up." Held in Toronto, Caribana has replaced Emancipation Day as the major Black event in the city.

The first parade route followed Yonge Street and ended at Nathan Phillips Square, then it moved to University Avenue in 1970 and remained there until 1991, when it was relocated to Lakeshore Boulevard. Some of the islands represented are Trinidad, Jamaica, Barbados, and the Bahamas. The South American country of Brazil is also included. Parades consist of hours of masquerade

A steel pan band playing on a parade float for Caribana. The steel pan is a percussion instrument. It originated in Trinidad and Tobago in the 1930s when the tops of petroleum oil drums were cut and hammered out to make different musical notes.

Courtesy of Hameed Shaqq.

bands, vibrant costumes, and steel bands. The music includes calypso, soca, reggae, R&B, and hip hop. Thousands of people enjoy West-Indian music, art, and food over the civic holiday long weekend. Other Caribana activities include competitions, boat cruises, dances, and concerts. The festival is a big financial boost to Toronto, bringing almost five hundred million dollars into the economy.[7]

Several junior Caribana parades were introduced in Toronto in the 1990s to provide an opportunity for youth of all backgrounds to connect to Caribbean culture through music, costume, and dance. They traditionally take place one week before the main Caribana parade.

ALL DRESSED UP WITH SOMEWHERE TO GO

The grandeur of Emancipation Day required that men and women dress their best. How they looked and presented themselves was important. Wearing their finest clothes, their "Sunday Best," was an expression of freedom, because enslaved Blacks had not been permitted to wear certain clothes. The slave master provided clothing, usually once a year. It was often old, tired hand-me-downs or clothing made from coarse fabric such as burlap, and sometimes shoes were not included. At Emancipation Day events, the dress was often formal and glamorous. Men and women chose to wear elaborate and extravagant suits and dresses to symbolize their status as free persons and to express themselves in as masculine or feminine a way as they desired.

Processionists wore sophisticated uniforms and ornate costumes. Celebrants dressed in holiday garb. They had their outfits specially made, or purchased them in special shops. The local newspapers provided detailed accounts on how Emancipation Day excursionists were dressed. In 1859 the *Hamilton Spectator* noted, "... our colored lady friends displayed, yesterday, the most effulgent robes, the most splendid silks and satins, that can be seen in a day's shopping."[8] In 1907 in Ingersoll, a town in Oxford County in southwestern Ontario, women wore "fine hooped skirts" and men dressed in "white vests, full dress coat, peg-top

trousers, and white neck-tie with elaborate stand-up collars."[9] The *Brantford Weekly Expositor* described how ladies looked lovely from their feet to their heads: "Young women robed in floor sweeping gowns of salmon pink and royal blue raise delicate gloved hands, to their coiffed ringlets."[10] The men were portrayed as wearing "black frock coats, light pants, white vests, and black plug hats."[11] Their exceptionally neat dressing during the mid to late nineteenth century showed the civility of Blacks and reflected their elevated social standing.

Emancipation Day celebrations received media coverage in newspapers across the country.

Courtesy of the *Chatham Daily News*.

In the twentieth century, donning the latest fashion during August First festivities remained popular. During the 1930s, ladies dressed in lace-trimmed dresses, butterfly skirts, and sailor suits, while gentlemen looked sharp in zoot suits. African Canadians continued to attend Emancipation Day in the 1940s and 1950s, well-dressed in peep toe shoes, gloves, puppy skirts,

Beehive hairstyles, a-line skirts, empire-line dresses, slim-fit pants, and Mary Jane shoes with bobby socks. Men sported flannel suits and penny loafers.

The 1960s saw an evolution of fashion that reflected the revolutionary sentiments and racial pride of the Civil Rights Movement and an emerging middle class and urban culture. Ladies wore mini-skirts, psychedelic prints, highlighter colours, pillbox hats, sleeveless shift dresses, skinny jeans, pleated skirts, and patent leather or vinyl shoes and handbags. Men wore buffalo plaid shirts and unisex fashions, such as bell-bottom jeans, blue jeans, and dashikis. Both genders widely embraced what the afro symbolized — pride in one's African identity. In the following decades, celebrants continued to wear trendy but less formal clothing. The clothing reflected the social attitudes of the time, as more liberal and inclusive ideals of youth led to different styles of dress.

Every year African Canadians were marching toward freedom, celebrating the freedom that was achieved so far, and taking steps toward the freedom yet to be fulfilled. The involvement of youth in the most anticipated event of Emancipation Day — the parade — ensured the longevity of the tradition. Emancipation Day parades were important, effective in the public expression of and petition for freedom.

CHAPTER SEVEN

LEISURE TIME: THERE'S FUN TO BE HAD BY ALL

Everybody's dancin', come on, let's go see,
Peace in the valley, now they want to be free.
— "PEOPLE GOT TO BE FREE," THE RASCALS, 1968.

After church services and parades, there were other important aspects of the commemoration: recreational and entertainment activities. Day-to-day, there were generally few public places where Blacks could feel welcome or were allowed to frequent. Furthermore, people often spent long hours working. So this portion of the day or weekend was highly valued, because it provided the opportunity for camaraderie among family, local citizens, and visitors. People of different racial, economic, and social backgrounds played, ate, and partied together, building community networks.

Afternoon leisure programs were an opportunity to have spontaneous fun. Adults and children alike could participate in sports. Attendees could see talented performers, entertainers, and artists from other countries or parts of the provinces. It was also an occasion for the reunion of African-Canadian families who may have been separated by distance.

PICNICS

Outdoor excursions took place at public parks and fairgrounds after the religious services and street processions. Emancipation Day gatherings were held at Exhibition Park, in Toronto; Agriculture Park and Mohawk Park, in Brantford; Lagoon Park, in Sandwich; Dundurn Park, in Hamilton; Sunset Point Park, in Collingwood; Cadboro Bay, on Vancouver Island; and Town Park, in Amherstburg. Many of these locations included beaches along the shores of the Great Lakes and had carnival rides and large playing fields.

Picnics were community-oriented, organized by churches and social organizations, often on an annual basis. Families organized picnics as yearly get-togethers. These outings — another form of giving thanks to God for the abundance in their lives and for the degree of freedom that Blacks enjoyed as citizens of Canada — were usually scheduled on the Emancipation Day weekend.

Before Owen Sound Emancipation Day celebrations were centralized in Harrison Park in 1912, the picnics were hosted by the Owen Sound (Little Zion) BME Church. Church parishioners and community members took steamers across Georgian Bay to Leith, Presque Isle, and Balmy Beach. At one particular outing at Presque Isle, two elderly Black men shared personal recollections about slavery in the United States. One was Thomas Henry Miller, the pastor of the BME church and the son of a slave. The second man was Jim "Old Man" Henson, a resident of Owen Sound who was an escaped slave from Maryland and whose life story was first published in *Broken Shackels*, in 1889.

St. Paul's AME Church in Hamilton organized a picnic to observe the 56th anniversary of the Slavery Abolition Act. Approximately three hundred people took the ferry boat from Hamilton to Bayview Park, located on the shores of Lake Ontario near Macassa Bay, to participate in the outing. An evening program was held at the church, with a festive dinner and performances by the children.

Between 1923 and 1935, the Montreal division of the Universal Negro Improvement Association (UNIA) scheduled their annual picnic to coincide with Emancipation Day celebrations. On August 2, 1923, about 350 men, women, and children travelled to Otterburn Park, located approximately sixteen kilometres south of Montreal, on a hired Canadian National Railway train. At the park, they played sports and games, danced, sang, and ate.

This photo is of community elder Paul "Dad" Lewis and two young children at Springbank Park in London, Ontario, in 1959. Paul was involved in celebrations in London for over fifty years as a member of the organizing committee, a participant, and a spectator. Emancipation Day family picnics have been held at Springbank since 1926.

SPOTLIGHT ON …

Oscar and Leona Brewton
moved to Toronto from
Emerson, Ohio, shortly after
the First World War. They
started a care clinic on Yonge
Street. Mr. Brewton was a
podiatrist, offering specialized foot care in his Comfort
Clinic. Mrs. Brewton operated
a beauty school and hair salon
and was very active in working
with Black youth. The couple
were longstanding members of
the First Baptist Church.

At High Park in Toronto, Leona Brewton, also known as Madame Brewton, and her husband, podiatrist Dr. Oscar Brewton, hosted an Emancipation Day picnic on the first Thursday in August throughout the 1930s. That particular date was chosen like the date for the "Big Picnic" in St. Catharines had been — to accommodate the working schedule of Black domestics, who usually received the first Thursday of the month off. Over one hundred people always attended.

Grimsby Park, located along the shores of Lake Ontario between Hamilton and St. Catharines, was another popular destination in the early 1900s for Emancipation Day celebrations. By the 1920s, it was the largest amusement park in Ontario, including a big midway with many attractions (carousels, roller coasters, a ferris wheel) and a roller-skating rink. There were cottages surrounding the lakeside park. One Grimsby resident recalls huge crowds of African Canadians coming in to town each summer and that the gatherings were accompanied by a great deal of dancing and merriment. The resident recalled that everyone enjoyed these events, "especially the wonderful music of the jubilee singers who pour their hearts in rhythm and song."[1]

Ray Lewis was one of the celebrants at Grimsby Park. He remembered going to Grimsby Park as a young boy with his family and fellow members of St. Paul's AME church. The annual picnic grew each year and was eventually moved to Port Dalhousie in St. Catharines by 1924.

In the twentieth century, Emancipation Day was generally commemorated in a more relaxed atmosphere, and it grew to a more picnic-style celebration in many locations. Some of the traditional aspects were done away with, and there was more emphasis on having a good time. The special weekend became a community family reunion, or a homecoming.

After the Civil War ended and American slavery was abolished, some African Americans who had settled in Canada, or their descendants, repatriated to the United States to reunite with family and take advantage of the opportunities that were sure to open up there for Blacks. African Canadians also moved to America in the decades after the Civil War in search of education and employment opportunities that were not open to them in Canada because of their race. For Emancipation Day, throngs of family members eagerly returned to the towns and cities where they grew up or where their extended family had lived for a long time. They looked forward to reuniting with family and friends. At these picnics, little cousins, who seldom saw each other during the year, played together. The picnics, which might include a barbeque cookout, outdoor games, speeches, and other forms of entertainment, were without a doubt the best place to go for reuniting with friends.

People brought picnic baskets filled with appetizing food — sandwiches, drinks, fried chicken, salads, and baked goods like cakes, pies, and breads, made especially for the day. Extended families and close friends also came together to put on huge Southern-styled barbeques, artfully grilling delicious barbeque chicken, ribs, and steak, and roasting corn and other vegetables on the grill in open barbeque pits. Watermelon, cotton candy, candy apple and other delectables were also on the menu. Regular visitors looked forward to the mouth-watering food that some ate only at this time of year.

The recipe for the barbeque sauce used at Jackson Park in Windsor was top secret. Passed down for generations, it was made by Windsorite Sarah Horn during the 1950s and 1960s, a relative of organizer Walter Perry. The recipe was kept in a different undisclosed place each year, and Mrs. Horn was even offered $2,000 for it. Her son, Ray Horn, was a regular barbeque chef at Jackson Park. During the

> —The Bartons, a colored family, who lived near Pine Grove, many years ago, and who, with their relatives in Toronto now number about 200 persons, have been granted the use of the Agricultural Society's grounds for Emancipation Day and the week following. It is their intention to hold a big picnic and camp there for a week.

The Barton family lived in Chinguacousy, now part of Brampton, Ontario. Levi Barton Sr. worked as a day labourer for Thomas and William Montgomery of Montgomery Inn in Etobicoke, Ontario, and often purchased food items from them. Levi Barton Jr. and other family members lived on Centre Street in Toronto, which had a large number of Black residents. Levi Jr. came in third place for the run, hop, step, and jump race in 1892 at the August First gathering at the Exhibition Park in Toronto.

From the *Brampton Conservator*, June 3, 1898.

1950s and 1960s, as much as four tons of ribs and two thousand chickens were cooked over the weekend.

Picnics have also been part of Caribana in Toronto. Thousands of people converge on Toronto Centre Island over three days to participate in all of the same activities.

Annual picnics were a time for enjoyment and fellowship. Friends and family would meet and catch up on what had gone on during the past year and share personal stories. They spent hours storytelling and laughing together. They also enjoyed games and music together.

SPORTS

There were all kinds of races at Emancipation Day: the three-legged race, the potato sack race, the hopping race, the ½ hour race, hop, step, and jump, the 100 yards dash, the fat men's race, the ½ mile race, the 300 yards race, the ladies 50 yard race, the oddfellows race, and the married and single men's races were just some of the racing competitions. Races were organized according to age groups, such as twelve and under, and organized by gender or marital status — boys, girls, old men, and single ladies.

A wide array of contests captured the interests of the diverse crowd and included horseshoeing, greasy pig contests, greasy pole climbing, tug-of-war, high jumping, the oldest person and the youngest person in attendance, the person who travelled the farthest, various band contests, and the popular the Miss Sepia International Pageant beauty contest.

The Miss Sepia pageant in Windsor attracted large numbers of contestants from Canada and the United States. Girls of African descent displayed their beauty and talents, and contestants were judged on evening gowns, swimwear, and talent. The dark-hued beauties rode on floats that travelled along the parade route. Crowned winners also won cash prizes, trophies, flowers, and a special photo shoot. The contenders received coverage, which included photo in the newspapers.

A children's three-legged race at the 2005 Emancipation Festival in Owen Sound.

Courtesy of Cherylyn Hansler.

Little Miss Sepia contest was added for young girls to participate. The Miss Sepia contest was introduced in Toronto in 1964 at commemorations held at Victoria Memorial Park. The first winner was seventeen-year-old Nerene Grizzle, who remembers feeling pleasantly surprised when her name was announced. She still has the trophy today![2]

Many young girls vied for the Miss Sepia title because it was one of the few platforms open to them for this kind of competition. Most of the twentieth-century Black women were not allowed to enter mainstream beauty pageants and were not featured in magazines, commercials, or print advertisements. Nerene recalls, "I understood from the organizers that I was then expected to be a contestant in the Miss Canada Pageant. It was devastating to be told later that I was being denied entry because at that time, apparently a Black girl would not be allowed to compete."[3] Another recognition for older African-Canadian women was the title of Queen of Emancipation Day, which was given at some annual picnics, including the one in Owen Sound.

There were also various skills competitions, such as baton twirling, boxing, best needlework, and the prettiest quilt, to name a few.

Prior to the First World War, Emancipation Day races and contests were usually limited to Blacks, but exceptions were made for interested Whites, as was the case for Mr. John White, a lawyer at Chatham's commemoration of the seventy-first anniversary of the Slavery Abolition Act. "The program clearly stated that the fat man's race was reserved for colored men only, but when the committee saw the look of disappointment on Mr. White's countenance when he read the bill, they decided to throw the race open to any fat man ... He ran so well that he won the race, also the prize — a box of cigars."[4]

Baseball, a favourite recreational pastime in North America from the mid-1850s to almost the end of the twentieth century, was another popular feature of Emancipation Day commemorations: "... a very enjoyable time was spent in a game of baseball in which both the young men and women took part."[5] Informal groups and professional teams played baseball matches. Young boys, men, and young girls formed teams for the day, local community teams participated, and all-Black clubs made up of trained baseball players also played. The St. Catharines Bulldozers, the Chatham Colored All Stars, and the London Colored Stars were a few of the professional African-Canadian baseball teams that were part of segregated

SPOTLIGHT ON ...

Nerene Virgin (née Grizzle) is a former television personality. She is the daughter of Stanley Grizzle (see page 58). On her mother's side, her great-uncle was John Christie Holland, the son of escaped slaves. John was the pastor for St. Paul's AME Church in Hamilton (now called Stewart Memorial) and was a well-known leader in Hamilton's Black community in the early 1900s.

Here is last year's Queen of Beauty, Miss International Sepia, and her two gorgeous handmaidens. The annual contest for the coveted title is the greatest of its kind in America. No other contest attracts such lovely girls. None other offers such prizes. None other carries with it such prestige. Left to right are Miss Beverly Evans, second; Miss Mary Clarke, Miss International Sepia; and Miss Cora Davis, third. Miss Clarke, by winning, became a member of Sigma Phi Kappa, world's most exclusive, most beautiful sorority.

The crowned 1949 Miss Sepia International, centre, accompanied by the runner-ups.

Courtesy of the E. Andrea Shreve Moore Collection, Essex County Black Historical Research Society.

provincial leagues. By the 1880s African Canadians were barred from playing in the White professional leagues, and, as a result, they established their own barnstorming baseball league and teams, touring on baseball circuits through rural areas for exhibition games.

However, Emancipation Day provided for a somewhat racially integrated exchange. Blacks played against Whites, but there were no teams mixed with players of both races: "In the afternoon a baseball match in which the local colored nine, the Northern Stars, swamped a picked team of white players caused

The St. Catharines Bulldozers baseball team played in the 1940s and 1950s in their home town and played in other places in Ontario such as Hamilton and Brantford. Circa 1950s. Players in the back row, left to right: Chester Smith, Amos Dorsey, Charles Dorsey, Richard Harper, Harry Harper. Middle row, left to right: George Bell, Les Bell, Bob Bell. Front: Ralph Bell.

Courtesy of the St. Catharines Museum, N9080.

many a dusky son to show his ivory, and give other more audible expressions of delight."[6] It provided a venue where Blacks could laugh at Whites and shout out comments without any fear of racial reprisal. Baseball games were often exciting and spectacular, at times lasting for two or three hours.

Other organized sports played during August First included lacrosse — one of Canada's two official sports — and soccer. The *Dresden Times* describes how well the ball and lacrosse games were played at Tecumseh Park in Chatham, with Chatham winning the baseball match and Windsor being victorious in the lacrosse game.[7] According to personal accounts, there was a yearly soccer game between local Black and White teams in Oro, Simcoe County, located between Barrie and Orillia, that drew many observers: "The negroes were skilled at hitting the ball with their heads and sending it great distances. Their weak spots were their shins, a fact that their opponents kept in mind."[8] As decades passed, baseball teams and games became more racially mixed, reflecting the increasing biracial make up of celebrants.

Rides were huge attractions, and by the turn of the twentieth century, they were a growing form of mass entertainment. Some of the parks had fairground rides and carnival games. For example, Lakeside Park in St. Catharines had a variety of rides, including the whirling ride called the Hey Day, an airplane ride, a merry-go-round, a carousel, and bumper cars. At other parks, midways were set up like at Jackson Park in Windsor. During the Depression Era, rides and games cost between five and ten cents each. Children and adults attending Emancipation Day festivities at public parks had a good time on these exciting attractions. People also enjoyed swimming, canoeing, rollerskating, playing card games, dominoes, and craps games.

Vendors set up shop at picnic sites, selling finely-made crafts and food items, such as baked goods, soda, barbecued meats, traditional African-American meals, and lemonade. It was an ideal opportunity to promote the work and products of African-Canadian artisans and for vendors to earn an income. Black women would often sell needlework, baked goods, and preserves. Twentieth century August First marketplaces expanded to include books, T-shirts, paintings, and other works of art. Caribana viewers could be tempted along the parade route or at Toronto Centre Island with Caribbean cuisine, including jerk chicken, roti, seasoned roasted corn, roasted fish, cook up rice, black pudding, and coconut water.

Of course, a wonderful day outdoors would not be complete without music. The day included park concerts by local and American church choirs, community choirs, and bands. Everyone enjoyed the playing and singing of hymns, traditional spirituals, anti-slavery music, and folksongs. Instrumental bands played throughout the day, and singers performed in the open air. The young and the old danced into the evening sunset.

EVENING FESTIVITIES

Emancipation Day carried on well into the night, with a host of activities and entertaining programs. Church services, parades, and picnics were followed by sumptuous banquets and a night filled with a variety of entertainment, such as dramatic and musical performances.

Jephtha and His Daughter, a cantata (a type of musical play), was performed in Hamilton in 1906 under the direction of S.R. Overstreet, who at that time was the basso singer for the Famous Canadian Jubilee Singers. A popular freedom celebration pageant called *Ethiopia at the Bar of Justice*, which featured spirituals, African history, and themes of enslavement, emancipation, and the ongoing fight for equality was staged as part of Emancipation Day in Windsor in 1954. The inclusion of theatrical performances served to teach viewers about history, political affairs related to people of African descent, and values, with the aim of improving community development and uplifting the African race. They were big productions designed to create the opportunity for youth and adults to become involved as actors and set creators.

To cap off celebrations, a grand ball or dance was held. Black men and women, including some Whites, wearing elaborate dresses and suits, danced to the music furnished by live bands and performers, partying into the late hours of the night. There was music of all kinds at Emancipation Day celebrations: gospel choirs, classical soloists, duet singers, R&B singers, and opera groups from local Canadian towns and from across the American border. Up to the beginning of the First World War, brass bands were popular because it was the music of the time, and this included operettas, waltzes, and marches. The 1880s and 1890s witnessed the rise of Black popular music, such as ragtime, rhythm and blues, and jazz. Soul music became the standard in the mid-1950s. The various forms of Black music were spiritually based, strongly influenced by traditional church songs.

Big band leader Tommy Earlls, of the band Tommy Earlls and His International Untouchables, playing the trumpet at Owen Sound's Emancipation Festival in 2005.

Courtesy of Cherylyn Hansler.

These annual Emancipation Day recitals provided a venue for Black musicians and their work. For instance, the O'Banyoun Jubilee Singers, founded in the 1860s by Josephus O'Banyoun in Halifax, Nova Scotia, and its offspring the Famous Canadian Jubilee Singers, — established in about 1879 in Hamilton, Ontario, by Josephus — performed regularly on Emancipation Day. Both groups were jubilee chorus ensembles accompanied by brass orchestra and other instruments.

Poster of the Famous Canadian Jubilee Singers lithograph, 1902. The world renowned performers toured Canada, the United States, and Europe.

Courtesy of Library and Archives Canada, Andrew Audobon Merrilees fonds, e002712912.

The music and influence of African-Canadian composers and singers in North America was evident at annual events. Ragtime and jazz songs written by Robert Nathaniel Dett of Niagara were performed. Shelton Brooks, who was born in Amherstburg and lived in North Buxton as a child, and North Buxton native Louis "Lou" Hooper frequently performed as part of Emancipation Day programs. Their work gained international recognition when they all moved to the United States to pursue their music careers. Singers like sopranos Carlotta Franzel and Grace Bumbry performed many times at Windsor's "Greatest Freedom Show on Earth." Carlotta, born Pauline McCaughan in Buxton, made her professional singing debut in the 1943 production of the Broadway play *Carmen Jones* as Cindy Lou, and Grace gained worldwide acclaim for her vocal abilities.

Countless August First performances were held at bandstands such as Jackson Park in Windsor, where the Detroit Negro Civic Opera Company, gospel group Clara Ward and the Ward Singers, and numerous up-and-coming motown artists captivated gigantic crowds.

The inclusion of a spectrum of Black music to mark Emancipation Day demonstrates its power and ability to unify people, to express collective feelings of love, peace, and happiness, and reflect beauty, hope, and promise in times of suffering, injustice, and sometimes even violence.

People strutted their stuff in the latest dances. And boy, did they ever dance! Celebrants burned up the dance floor with the latest dances. The cakewalk was a popular dance competition at Emancipation Day festivals during the nineteenth century. Originating from enslaved African Americans in southern plantations, the dance required couples to bow and bend while doing a high-step promenade, a basic dance move of walking steps and figures, typically involving a high prance with a backward tilt. They would parade and prance around a designated square-dance area, keeping time with the music. The dancers strutted and did flamboyant kicks and intricate spins and turns so the judges could evaluate them on their style, poise, precision, and uniqueness of moves. The winning couple took home a beautifully decorated cake, hence the phrase "taking the cake."

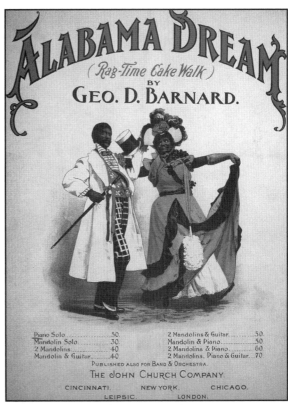

The cover of sheet music for Alabama Dream Rag-Time Cake Walk. Ragtime music was composed by African-Canadian musicians including Robert Nathaniel Dett, Shelton Brooks, and William C. Handy and was often featured at Emancipation Day observances.

Courtesy of the Hopkins University Lester S. Levy Collection of Sheet Music, Box 170, Item 170.005.

Typical of the high calibre of entertainment which has always been a feature of every Emancipation Day celebration at Windsor, Ontario, is the Detroit Negro Opera Chorus shown above. Sunday evening programs have always been a pageant of colorful singing by groups of highly-trained singers, and deep devotional services. The committee in charge of this portion of the program has always obtained the highest type of entertainment.

The Detroit Negro Civic Opera Company was comprised of highly trained singers. The group was organized and directed by Jerene Gurley Macklin, who also conducted Windsor's Emancipation Day music program in the 1940s and 1950s.

Courtesy of the E. Andrea Shreve Moore Collection, Essex County Black Historical Research Society.

Our Thanks . . .

The British American Association of Colored Brothers extends its heartfelt appreciation to individuals and groups whose assistance has helped us immeasurably in staging this year's Emancipation Day celebration. It is impossible to mention each individually, but we would like to single out The Windsor Daily Star, the staffs of the Ambassador Bridge and the Detroit-Windsor Tunnel, Radio Station CK-LW, the Detroit and Windsor immigration and customs departments, the press of the United States, the Windsor Police and Fire Departments, the St. Johns Ambulance Corps, the Legion of Frontiersmen, and fraternal organizations of both Canada and the United States.

REV. ADAM CLAYTON POWELL, JR.

Rev. Adam Clayton Powell, Jr., has twice consented to be our featured speaker. Rev. Powell is one of the best-known speakers of the Race. He is America's third Negro United States congressman, pastor of the Abyssinia Baptist Church of New York City, the former director of relief in Harlem, and chairman of the co-ordinating committee which won employment for Negroes with the New York Bus Company, former member of the Consumer Division Committee of the O.P.A., the All-Harlem Victory Council. Rev. Powell is the husband of Hazel Scott, famous pianist.

In the evening, hundreds went down to see the promised cake walk for the cake put up by 'Mistah John Miglochum.' The pavilion was crowded with visitors. Bashfulness, however, delayed the commencement of the dancing until after 10 o'clock. After a couple of sets, two little girls, Inez Roy, daughter of William Roy, and Maudie Mason, daughter of John Mason, commenced the cake walk and were loudly applauded. The former then retired and Ollie Boohey took her place. Two older girls, Rosa Mason and Nellie Wesley also entered the competition. The dancing of all the girls was good and graceful, though the absence of male partners detracted from its effect. The judge, Mr. Jack Emslie, awarded the prize to little Maudie Mason. The decision met with general approval, which was evidenced by a hearty applause, as the little one bore proudly away her cake.[9]

Other trendy nineteenth-century dances included tangos, two steps, marches, and waltzes.

Some early twentieth-century dance styles were the grizzly bear, the turkey trot, the bunny hug, and the Charleston. Swing dances like the lindy hop and the jitterbug were all the rage in the 1940s and 1950s. During this same era, people played music on jukeboxes and danced the night away. Emancipation Day partygoers had a pleasurable time expressing themselves through dance.

Occasionally, gun salutes were given, cannons fired, and firework displays lit up the night sky in ceremonial honour of the abolition of slavery. "Early in the morning, almost at break of day, twenty-one rounds were fired from cannons stationed at the extreme point of the military ground; near to which spot was created an arbour of boughs about sixty feet long."[10] The grand celebration hosted in Toronto in 1854 closed with a colourful firework show. These ceremonies were part of the public statement of African Canadians about their feelings on the abolition of slavery.

Emancipation Day celebrations provided a fun-filled afternoon and an evening or weekend of enjoyment. Families, friends, and neighbours delighted in appetizing picnics. Leisure activities and performances provided an opportunity to showcase the outstanding skills and talents of many African Canadians in sports, music, and drama. There was a wide range of engaging activities that attracted young people. As celebrations grew to be more elaborate and complex over time, there was more emphasis on socializing and popular entertainment. In some form or another, leisure activities have always been a part of Emancipation Day, another symbolic way to express freedom.

CHAPTER EIGHT

ORAL CULTURE AND EMANCIPATION DAY: TALKING ABOUT FREEDOM

*Talking about freedom, talking about freedom,
we will fight for the right to live in freedom.*
— "Freedom," Paul McCartney, *Driving Rain*, Capital Records, 2001.

Speeches were an integral component of Emancipation Day commemorations. In the 1800s, speeches were an important form of education because of the low levels of literacy. Few people could read or write, especially among formerly enslaved Africans who had been denied access to a formal education. An oral culture developed, which was essential for communicating and preserving history and cultural values, as well as bringing public awareness to pertinent issues of the time. Speeches were also a form of entertainment and drew on the importance of the oral tradition in African culture. While discussing serious topics, humour was incorporated as well as aspects of church sermons. The "call and response" was utilized to hold the attention of the audience.

A spectrum of speakers were invited to talk at various venues, including churches, parks, mechanic institutes, and community and private halls were filled with individuals both Black and White, male and female, from assorted professions and backgrounds. [1] Storytelling by community elders became an important aspect of the oral traditions of August First. Organizers invited speakers who remembered slavery because they were once enslaved or because they could share the experiences of older relatives who were once enslaved. In 1952 the *Windsor Daily Star* announced, "An unusual treat will be the appearance of Rev. William Harrison of Windsor, who will speak Sunday afternoon. He is 87 and the oldest living resident who can recall the days of slavery."[2] Reverend Harrison, the minister of the BME church in Windsor, was an annual *griot* — the term for a respected traditional West-African storyteller — at Jackson Park since 1935. He talked about the early freedom seekers who journeyed to Canada. Perhaps the newspaper called his appearance unusual because it was rare at that time for the public receive such rich first-hand information. He had been born in London, Ontario, on February 24, 1866. His mother was Isabelle Nelson Harrison, a free Black woman from Kentucky, and his father was Thomas Harrison, a fugitive slave from Missouri. His brother, Richard B. Harrison, also born in London, became a famous actor in the United States. He performed in the Broadway play called *The Green Pastures*, which ran from 1930 to 1935.

Abolitionists, many of whom were church ministers, spoke about the moral evil of the enslavement of Africans and the urgent need to abolish the inhumane practice. Reverend William King, founder of the Elgin Settlement in Buxton, delivered a sermon at an Emancipation Day church service in Chatham in 1856, which he mentioned in his diary. In 1858 he spoke at Tecumseh Park on the state of slavery in the southern United States: "I hope the day is not far distant before this foul blot shall be wiped off from the national escutchion. The institution is doomed to destruction. Slavery cannot always last, it is in direct violation of the laws of God and the natural rights of man — a spirit of uneasiness is manifesting itself."[3] Reverend King referred to the increased agitation to end slavery in the South that would lead to the Civil War. Picnicking and dancing followed in the barracks. Other White ministers who participated in Emancipation Day included ministers from Montreal: Henry Wilkes, John McKillican, John McVicar, and Alex Kemp, who delivered sermons in the 1860s, as well as the men listed in the White Celebrants section in Chapter 4.

Lecturers often expressed patriotic sentiments toward Britain for ending slavery and gratitude to Canada for being a place of refuge to fugitives. In Montreal Alexander Grant, an African-American self-employed launderer who had come from New York four years earlier, asked his audience in Montreal on August 1, 1834 (the date the Slavery Abolition Act took effect), to "join [him] heart and hand in giving [their] warmest acknowledgements to Great Britain for the noble act she has performed." He went on to point out the privileges freed bondsmen and bondswomen could now embrace "under the protection of the British flag."[4] In 1847 in Windsor, Black abolitionist and newspaper publisher Henry Bibb, in addressing a group of recent fugitives, said, "… now you are in Canada, free from American slavery; yes the very moment you stept upon these shores you were changed from articles of property to human beings."[5]

Racial discrimination was another recurring topic that Emancipation Day orators tackled. In 1871 Robert L. Holden commented on the increase in racial prejudice against Blacks in Canada, particularly in Ontario and British Columbia. Robert argued that African Americans, who were only recently freed from slavery, were progressing better socially and politically than African Canadians who obtained liberty first. Robert L. Holden was also one of several speakers in Chatham in 1891 who focused their attention on denouncing the unacceptable level of racism Blacks in Ontario were facing in sending their children to public schools, employment, housing, serving on jury, and receiving service in hotels and restaurants.

Reverend William King, founder of the Elgin Settlement and Buxton Mission, the most successful planned community for fugitive slaves. By the 1860s, over 400 Black families (about 2,000 people) owned land in Buxton and helped to build a thriving community.

Courtesy of the Buxton National Historic Site & Museum.

SPOTLIGHT ON ...

William King, a White Presbyterian minister and teacher, was living in Louisiana when he accepted a missionary position in Toronto in 1846. The following year, to his dismay, he inherited fourteen slaves from his wife's estate. William brought them back to Canada, including a young man whom he purchased, with the intention of freeing them all. He started the Elgin Settlement in Buxton, Ontario, to help former slaves to support themselves. Today the area is known as North Buxton and is recognized as a national historic site. The Buxton National Historic Site and Museum consists of one of the schools and a log cabin of the settlement, along with some of Reverend King's belongings. Descendants of original settlers continue to live in the community.

Guest speakers who were "race men," community activists concerned with the upliftment and betterment of the Black race, were always on the program. Prominent among them were Henry Bibb, in 1847 in Windsor; Frederick Douglass, in 1854 at the Dawn Settlement in Dresden; Martin R. Delany, in 1857 in Chatham; Josephus O'Banyoun, in 1878 in Hamilton, 1889 in Amherstburg, in Dresden in 1890, and in Chatham in 1891; Robert L. Holden, in 1871 and 1891 in Chatham, as well as 1895 in London; John Henry Alexander, in Amherstburg in 1894; and Stanley Grizzle, in Toronto in the 1950s. They encouraged social advancement of the African race through education, personal demonstration of integrity, and inspiring excellence.

Youth were often targeted by headline speakers, who encouraged them to pursue an education. Obtaining an education would ensure a better future for the individual, their family, and their community. In Amherstburg in 1889, Reverend E. North of Colchester South pointed out "the power of education to remove prejudices against their race, as it elevated them in all relations of life and qualified them to fill any position in the land." In Chatham in 1891, Josephus O'Banyoun suggested that Emancipation Day should be a time to celebrate what African Canadians should be and aspired to be. Orra L.C. Hughes, a Black lawyer from Pennsylvania, addressed the gatherers in Hamilton in 1878. He stated that any man who had an impact on the world acquired knowledge by some means and that knowledge would be an important tool for Blacks in dispelling myths of African inferiority while reclaiming their position as disciplined learners.

Black speakers consistently worked to instil racial pride and a sense of history among youth and adults by educating them about the development of African civilizations and Black contributions to Canada and the world. Black nationalists, people who believed in the necessity for unity among Africans around the world, used Emancipation Day speeches to encourage African nationalism. Marcus Garvey, founder and president of the Universal Negro Improvement Association, delivered a speech with a call to action in St. Catharines in 1938. While in Toronto for the Eighth International Convention of the Negro Peoples of the World, Garvey attended the annual picnic sponsored by the Toronto division of the UNIA at Lakeside Park, Port Dalhousie, in St. Catharines. Hundreds of people heard Garvey say, "The negro must take his place in the world before it is too late,"[6] referring to the necessity of people of African origin to have their own nation, to repatriate to Africa in order to ensure the survival of the race. Pan-Africanists pressed emigration out of North America to places in Africa or the Caribbean with Black majorities to attain equality.

African-American civil rights activists made up a large number of the speakers in the 1950s and 1960s, especially at events in Windsor. Martin Luther King Jr. spoke there in August 1956, just after helping to kick start the Montgomery Bus Boycott, which was triggered by the arrest of Rosa Parks. Based on the Jim Crow Laws in Alabama, Rosa was required to give up her seat on the bus if it was needed by a White person. However, Rosa refused and was arrested by the police. In a show of solidarity and in an effort to change the racist law, Blacks refused to take public transit if they were going to be limited to sitting at the back of the bus. After thirteen months, the boycott ended in December 1956 when the United States Supreme Court ruled that segregation on buses was illegal.

An audience of over 5,000 at Jackson Park heard Baptist minister Martin Luther King Jr. describe the birth of a new age of justice and freedom for all men, filled with hope and possibility. He asserted that "there can be no birth without growing and pains and labor pains." Dr. King was referring to the fervent fight against segregation that was occurring in the southern states and the slow changes towards equality and integration that were taking place. He then encouraged

Blacks to "prepare for the new age of freedom" and to "achieve excellency in the areas that [they lived] in."[7]

Civil rights leader Dr. Martin Luther King Jr., 1956. Dr. King travelled across America to advocate for equal rights for Blacks and the poor. In 1964 he was awarded the Nobel Peace Prize in acknowledgment of his non-violent movement in the fight for justice.

Courtesy of the E. Andrea Shreve Moore Collection, Essex County Black Historical Research Society.

Adam Clayton Powell Jr., a church minister and congressman from New York, delivered addresses in 1945 and 1954. At his first Emancipation Day appearance, Mr. Powell warned the 30,000 listeners,

> The war is not finished and we shall not celebrate V-E Day when Japan is finished. There is another V-E Day to be anticipated. The true V-E Day will come in the United States and Canada when we celebrate equality of the races. We march towards a second emancipation ... We must not cringe before those people who in the war were ready to allow us to shed our blood in the fight but who in peace wish to give us again the mops, pail, and the broom ... There is no one here who can stop the rendezvous of the Black man with his true freedom.[8]

V-E Day was Victory in Europe Day, on May 8, 1945, when the Second World War ended. He referred to the fact that Black men have fought for equality in several wars, but have yet to obtain it for themselves in their own countries. Other American civil rights speakers included Daisy Bates, an American civil rights activist; Reverend Fred Shuttlesworth, Baptist minister and civil rights activist in Birmingham, Alabama; and Mrs. Medgar "Myrlie" Evers, wife of slain civil rights activist Medgar Evers of Mississippi.

African-Canadian civil rights activists were also very involved as August First speakers. Daniel G. Hill, the first director of the Ontario Human Rights Commission, delivered an address at Victoria Memorial Park in Toronto in 1958 and discussed the historic role of African-Canadian associations in that city going back to the 1840s. George McCurdy, who was at that time the human rights administrator in Ottawa, spoke briefly at Harrison Park, Owen Sound, in 1970. George was one of the community leaders who led the fight to close the segregated schools in Ontario. The last segregated school was closed in Colchester, just south of Windsor, in 1965.

Up until the 1950s, the headline guest speakers invited to speak were all men. As a reflection of the change of the social status of women, they began to be featured speakers at Emancipation Day observances. Female speakers included former first lady Eleanor Roosevelt and Mary MCleod Bethune, both of whom addressed the crowds at Jackson Park in Windsor in 1954. Mary, an African-American civil

Violet King, left, in Calgary, Alberta with Bennie Smith and Roy Williams (second and third right), leaders of the Calgary branch of the International Brotherhood of Sleeping Car Porters. Asa Philip Randolph, president of the North American all-Black union presents Violet with a purse in recognition of her achievement as the first African-Canadian female lawyer.

Courtesy of Glenbow Archives and Museum, NA-5600-7757a.

rights activist, threw a challenge to the listeners; "We must do away with everything like segregation and discrimination where we have one man up and another down. We must build a world where every man is up and no man is down."[9] Wife of the former U.S. president Franklin Delano Roosevelt, Eleanor delivered the speech to close the four-day festival. She talked about the freedom movements around the world in countries such as India and China and the push for equal rights by women worldwide: "There is a need for unity in the human race. People must learn to play together, work together, and live together."[10] African-Canadian Violet King, a native of Alberta, was invited to be the featured speaker in Toronto in 1958. Four years earlier, Violet had earned the distinction of becoming the first Canadian-born Black female lawyer. On the 125th anniversary of the Slavery Abolition Act, Violet highlighted three recent accomplishments in Black Canadians' fight for equality: serving in integrated military units in the Second World War, the unionization of the Sleeping Car Porters, and the passage of anti-discriminatory legislation such as the Fair Employment Practices Act of 1951 and the Fair Accommodation Practices Act of 1954. She summarized that all of these victories helped to narrow the gap of racism.

African-Canadian politicians like Isaac Holden, Robert L. Dunn, Ovid Jackson, and Lincoln Alexander also addressed August First assemblies. [11] Chatham alderman Isaac Holden spoke in 1871 and 1882 in Chatham. In 1882 he discussed the

> philanthropy of Wilberforce and his contemporaries who sounded the first tocsin (warning signal) of freedom, for eight hundred thousand slaves. He also dealt with considerable spirit on the great emancipation in America which broke asunder the manacles of four million beings. He closed the address by urging his people to make the best of themselves and lose no opportunity to cultivate all the humanities, that their race might prove they were worthy the freedom given them.[12]

Windsor city councillor Robert L. Dunn delivered a speech in Windsor in 1895 and in Chatham in 1899.

Owen Sound's first Black mayor, Ovid Jackson, spoke in Amherstburg in 1983 at the North American Black Historical Museum's inaugural Emancipation Day commemoration. The Honourable Lincoln Alexander was the keynote speaker at Uncle Tom's Cabin Historic Site in Dresden in 2005 and 2006. He spoke about the racism he had experienced as a youth and as an adult growing up in Hamilton. Alexander was born in Hamilton and achieved recognition as a lawyer and politician. He was the first Black lieutenant-governor in Ontario, Canada's first Black member of Parliament, and the first Black cabinet minister. The former politician discussed how he overcame prejudice and how Canadians of various races have fought for equality in Ontario and across Canada. He encouraged people "to stand up and be counted and never let this sort of thing [slavery] happen again."[13]

At times, other faith leaders were asked to speak to Emancipation Day crowds. This illustrated the wide array of Canadians who fought for equality for all citizens. Rabbi Abraham Feinburg of Holy Blossom Temple in Toronto shared his insight on discrimination with those who gathered in 1964. He asserted that mankind would "destroy itself in racial conflict" if society and the world did not become colour blind. He urged listeners to see beyond the colour of someone's skin by being accepting of everyone.

Emancipation Day speakers were articulate and eloquent. Many delivered carefully prepared addresses, while others spoke unscripted but passionately, from the heart. The purpose of including speakers in festival programs was to educate, captivate, inspire, motivate, and mobilize the Black community. Additionally, orators helped to encourage youth to make a positive impact on the future

A poster of the featured speakers and performers at Windsor's 1954 celebration.

Courtesy of the E. Andrea Shreve Moore Collection, Essex County Black Historical Research Society.

and to fight for the end of slavery and various forms of racial discrimination. Speeches were literary entertainment, an extension of African spoken word, and a means of voicing the goals and concerns of Black Canadians. The speeches were often printed later as pamphlets for educational purposes.

TOASTS AND RESOLUTIONS

The toasts and resolutions at Emancipation Day gatherings were also meaningful elements of the African oral culture. A toast is a tribute or proposal of best wishes, good health, and success, offered to someone or a group, and can be marked by people raising glasses and drinking together. Well-wishers could also respond in agreement, like responding with "amen" to a delivered toast. This kind of interaction between the speaker and the listener is known as "call and response," which is another example of African oral tradition. The speaker and his or her message is affirmed by the giving of a favourable verbal response. A resolution is a formal expression of opinion by a group of people in a meeting. Both forms of speaking were used to show patriotism toward Britain and the Queen.

They also reflected how African Canadians embraced their new citizenship and the rights and privileges that came along with it. As well, toasts expressed messages to fellow White citizens that they, the Black citizens, were appreciative of the opportunities afforded to them, such as free soil, security from slavery, as well as education. They communicated that Blacks in Canadian provinces were good, productive citizens.

Proclamations and resolutions called upon the future and declared new beginnings. Resolutions would be passed to chart the course for political or social action for the year to come, expressing the issues important to Black cultural organizations and the community.

For example, these seven toasts were offered at the gathering in Toronto in 1854:

1. The Queen — three cheers

2. The army and navy of Great Britain — three cheers

3. The Governor General — three cheers

4. "*The Provincial Freeman*" — remarks by the president and three cheers

5. *Three cheers for the Toronto and Hamilton Bands*

6. Resolved, That we celebrate the 1st of August, 1855 at Hamilton

7. Concluding toast — "Our Wives and Sweethearts."[14]

The toasts proposed in Halifax, Nova Scotia, in 1855 showed the racial and global awareness of the long-established Black community. They acknowledged their African roots. Black Haligonians were loyal to their country and to the British crown. Further, the toast reflected their understanding of the necessity of an international coalition in attacking slavery:

1. *Africa* — the land of our fathers …

2. *The Queen* — God bless her. Long may she reign over a free and generous nation.

3. Prince Albert, Prince of Wales, and all the Royal Family.

4. *General Simpson, and the Allied armies in the Crimea* …

5. Sir Gaspard Le Marchant, Governor, and Commander-in-Chief, and the British Army.

6. Vice Admiral Fanshawe, and the British Navy.

7. *Wilberforce and Clarkson* — the noble advocates for African liberty.

8. The President and Abolition Society of Nova Scotia.

9. The health of the Abolition Society in Canada, Bermuda, and all the West India Islands, who assemble in honor of this day.

10. The Lord Bishop and the Clergy of Nova Scotia.'11th. The Mayor and Corporation.

12. The Press of Nova Scotia.

13. Lady Le merchant, and the fair daughters of Acadia.

14. Our next merry meeting.[15]

The collective declaration passed at Emancipation Day in 1896 in London, as noted by a newspaper, was as follows:

God bless the Baptists, continued the speaker.

"Amen."

GOD BLESS THE POLITICAL PARTIES.

"God bless the Conservatives."

"Amen."

"God bless the Reformers."

"Amen."

"Amen make Laurier a man that will protect this country and not give away its rights to the United States...."

"God bless England," shouted somebody in the crowd.

"God bless England for her protection, for every good act she has done. God bless the Queen who sits on the throne and rules so nobly for men of all nationalities and colors...."

"Three cheers for the Queen," concluded Mr. Bazie, and they were given.[16]

Toasts and resolutions kept to a similar format wherever they were delivered, and they were regularly printed in local newspapers. They were usually drafted by members of the organizing committee. This media publicity meant that White Canadians got to see that Blacks shared some of the same feelings, sentiments, and aspirations.

READINGS

Readings were a significant ritual of the usual August First program. For example, sections of the Slavery Abolition Act, the Emancipation Proclamation, and the Thirteenth Amendment would have been read to those in attendance. Laws that had a significant impact of the lives of people of African origin in North America were shared. The British Slavery Abolition Act of 1833 that was passed on August 28, 1833, for example, read, "Whereas divers persons are holden in Slavery within divers of His Majesty's Colonies, and it is just and expedient that all such Persons should be manumitted and set free ..."

The Emancipation Proclamation was officially issued on January 1, 1863. While it did not end slavery, it provided the anticipated outcome of the Civil War if the Union Army won:

> ... all persons held as slaves within any State or designated part of a State, the people thereof shall then be in rebellion against the United States, shall be then, thenceforward, and forever free ... I do order and declare that all persons held as slaves within said designated States, and parts of States, are, and henceforward shall be free; and that the Executive government of the United

States including the military and naval authorities thereof, will recognize and maintain the freedom of said persons.

The Thirteenth Amendment to the United States Constitution, enacted on January 31, 1865, abolished slavery in America. It took effect on December 18, 1865. Section one read, "Neither slavery nor involuntary servitude, except as punishment for crime whereof the party shall have been duly convicted, shall exist within the United States, or any place subject to their jurisdiction." This is some of what was imparted to listeners.

As time went on, other freedom laws that were passed in Canada and the United States were read, such as the Fourteenth and Fifteenth Amendments to the United States Constitution, the Fair Employment Practices Act of 1951, the Fair Accommodations Practices Act of 1954, the 1964 Civil Rights Act, and the Voting Rights Act of 1965.[17] Copies were often put on display as well. Readings of freedom documents were another way in which patriotism and thanksgiving were exhibited. After the Reconstruction Era (1865 to 1877), the years after the Civil War and the end of American slavery, Emancipation Day readings commemorated North American Blacks' entitlement to constitutional rights.

The literary works of Black authors, including books, essays, and poems, were often recited. Written pieces that emphasized collective feelings and emotions or personified relevant social concerns were selected. Sharing their work illustrated the success of Black writers.

The oral tradition feature of Emancipation Day was a vital part of the education of celebrants. The purpose was to pass on the history from one generation to the next to guarantee that the diverse history of Black peoples was kept alive. It armed African-Canadians with the ammunition needed to continue the fight for freedom and equality.

CHAPTER NINE

THE PURSUIT OF FREEDOM: THE STRUGGLE AGAINST RACISM AND DISCRIMINATION

No easy walk to freedom, no easy walk to freedom.
Keep on walking and we shall be free, That's how were gonna make history."
— "No Easy Walk to Freedom," Peter, Paul, and Mary,
No Easy Walk to Freedom, 1986.

The August First observances in emerging urban centres and smaller towns were an opportunity for newly freed slaves to demonstrate their patriotism and allegiance to the British crown and their gratitude for freedom in Canada. However, they soon realized that the passage of the Slavery Abolition Act was just the beginning of the global movement for full rights and equality for people of African heritage. Without a doubt, that movement included Canada. The struggle for equal civil rights began immediately after emancipation. Although Blacks were no longer enslaved and were free in a general sense, their lives were still restricted because of their race — true freedom was far from their grasp. Once they received their citizenship, African Canadians expected the right to own property, educate their children, and exercise full civil liberties, including the right to vote and to serve on juries. But that did not happen.

African Canadians faced many social and political issues well into the twentieth century. Racial segregation was prevalent in education. Throughout the 1800s, African-Canadian children could not attend local public schools and were forced to go to legally segregated schools, except in Toronto. In post-secondary education, Black women were prohibited from enrolling in nursing programs during the 1930s and 1940s. Blacks in Canada also dealt with residential racism, a practice that denied them the right to rent or own property in certain places. They were denied the right to purchase government-owned land in some towns. Black men's rights to vote and serve on juries were hindered because of their race.[1] Even though they could exercise these rights by law, the racist practices in some locales often prevented them from doing so.

Employment opportunities were limited for African Canadians. Most were relegated to positions as domestic servants, bellhops, general labourers, chauffeurs, sleeping car porters, railway construction workers, and farm help. Blacks were excluded from certain jobs and not considered for certain promotions. They were also refused service or offered segregated service and accommodation in public businesses, such as movie and concert theatres, golf courses, restaurants, hotels, dance halls, bars, parks, restrooms, community centres, barber shops, and swimming pools. People of African descent who wished to immigrate to Canada between the 1890s and the 1960s also faced discrimination. Blacks from the English-speaking Caribbean were not allowed into Canada, despite being from sister British Commonwealth countries.

By the 1940s, people of African ancestry had still not achieved complete equal rights in Ontario and other regions of Canada. The generally accepted view was that Blacks were not equal participants in the nation's democracy. This fuelled a Canadian civil rights movement that saw men and women of different racial groups — Blacks, Jews, Whites, and Aboriginals — join together to fight racism. These activists would later form the labour and human rights movement.

African Canadians remained proactive by forming community organizations that had a mandate to challenge the unfair treatment of Blacks and to seek redress for racism. The National Unity Association (NUA) was formed in Dresden, Ontario, in 1948 by a group of African-Canadian citizens seeking to address the mistreatment of Blacks. The UNIA had strong membership enrolment during this time period, with several branches across Ontario and many others in Canada at large. The Negro Citizenship Association of Toronto was founded in 1951 by Donald Moore and other community leaders to press the federal government to change discriminatory immigration practices.

Human rights activist and African-Canadian historian Daniel G. Hill and his wife Donna Hill, who also fought against discrimination, entered the movement for equal rights when they moved to Toronto in 1953 from Washington, D.C. As an interracial couple, they experienced racism firsthand in their new country. The Hills had a difficult time finding an apartment because landlords did not want to rent to a Black man and a White woman. Their experiences led them to join the efforts of labour and human rights organizations to pressure the Ontario government to enact province-wide anti-discrimination legislation. For years, these groups were documenting cases of racial discrimination across Ontario as proof for the need of legal intervention. In 1962 Daniel Hill became the first director of the Ontario Human Rights Commission (OHRC). The OHRC is a government agency that was established to fight discrimination in its many forms and to enforce the then-newly passed anti-discrimination laws. Later, in 1978, Daniel, his wife, and some close friends founded the Ontario Black History Society (OBHS) to educate the public about Black history in Ontario and Canada. One goal of the OBHS was to combat racism against blacks through education.[2]

> **SEGREGATED SCHOOLING**
>
> The last school to be legally desegregated in Ontario was in Colchester, Essex County, in 1965. In Guysborough, Nova Scotia, the last segregated school closed in 1983. Toronto was an exception, in that the doors of elementary schools and colleges were always open to Black students.

Employment remained a major issue for African Canadians well into the twentieth century, and they sought equal opportunities in the workplace. Having a decent paying job with some benefits was (and still is) part of an acceptable quality of life. Blacks were at the forefront of both the human rights and labour movements, because as one of the most marginalized groups in North America, racism had a big impact on their lives. Because of this racial discrimination, Emancipation Day was used as a platform to heighten public awareness of the racism faced by African Canadians. This international freedom movement incorporated issues of labour and human rights since it began in 1834. The issue of racism was common in messages imparted at commemorations.

In 1891 the Kent County Civil Rights League (KCCRL) organized the Emancipation Day observance in Chatham. Many members in attendance were descendants of fugitive slaves who had settled in Kent County. All the speakers were instructed by the master of ceremonies, James C. Richards, to talk about the racial discrimination faced by Blacks in Chatham — the reason for the formation of the organization that year. Garrison Shadd, Mary Ann Shadd's brother, was one of the speakers on the lineup. He stated that "the policy of centuries of oppression and the policy of to-day was to keep the colored people ignorant," referring to the hundreds of years of discrimination inflicted on people of African descent. [3]

Reverend W. Constantine Perry, pastor of Toronto's AME church in the 1940s and 1950s, used Emancipation Day radio addresses on CKEY to highlight racism. For example, he discussed what Black women were facing in the nursing field in cities such as Toronto and Windsor:

> Applications of colored girls with the needed qualifications for nurse training have been subtly rejected with unwarranted excuses and suggestions that colored applicants seek training in the U.S., he said. "The question in the mind of the unprejudiced is, why such discrimination? The Bible nowhere sanctions or

approves it. The sciences of biology and anthropology emphatically disprove race and blood superiority. History records that the Negro, through his ability, can be found in every field of endeavour, in science, religion, invention, philosophy, music and other branches, with much distinction.[4]

As was the case in other regions of the country, Blacks in British Columbia faced segregation. African Canadians were not allowed to swim in city pools. Like other visible minority groups, they were subjected to discrimination in employment, housing, and public services. It should be no surprise, then, that the use of Emancipation Day to champion equal rights causes was evident in other parts of Canada. In 1961 the British Columbia Association for the Advancement of Coloured people (BCAACP) resurrected the August First commemorations in order to bring attention to the civil rights struggle. During the same decade, persistent American racism reached a peak, culminating in several riots across the country. One conflict in particular, the Detroit Riots of 1967, had an unfortunate consequence on Windsor's "Greatest Freedom Show on Earth." Since Detroit was Windsor's sister city, there were safety and security concerns in both cities, and the event's organizer, Walter Perry, was forced to cancel that year's week-long festival, as Windsor would not issue the necessary permits.

Emancipation Day's discussions of the challenges facing Blacks continued in the twenty-first century. In his speech delivered at Uncle Tom's Cabin Historic Site in 2005, Lincoln Alexander pointed out that "there's always needs to be vigilant about racism," noting "that's why legislation such as the Canadian Race Relations Act is in place."[5]

At times, African Canadians have experienced racism while observing Emancipation Day. In an incident in Seacliff Park in Leamington, Ontario, on August 4, 1930, approximately three hundred members of the three Black churches in Chatham — the Community Church (originally the Chatham

BME Church Victoria Chapel), the Campbell AME Church, and the First Baptist Church — were asked by Mayor Rodell Smith and the two city councillors to leave the park. It seems as though several White picnickers left Seacliff Park and made angry calls to the mayor because of the presence of Blacks in this public place, especially during the Civic Holiday weekend. Apparently, the picnickers were upset because the church members had broken a local tradition "which prevents colored people from making a rendezvous of the town or township or holidaying at the Park, especially on a public holiday."[6] It was agreed between the unwelcomed visitors and the representative of the town that they would leave by six o'clock in the evening. Such Jim Crow practices, although not found in writing, did exist in parts of Canada, including Essex and Chatham-Kent counties.[7] Ironically, this act of racism happened when a group of African Canadians most certainly planned their Sunday School Union picnic to coincide with the celebration of freedom to their long weekend outing.

In response to this blatant act of racism, the churches held a community meeting the following day. Reverend Charles Peyton Jones, pastor of the Campbell AME Church and organizer of the picnic, publicly expressed the group's frustration:

> We hold very strongly ... that Canada is a free country, and that in such a country no colored line should be drawn. No country is free where the colored line is drawn. As citizens of Canada our sons fought and died for it in the late World War. today, as citizens of the same country, we ask that tolerance and mutual good will toward all be the motto which will guide us towards a bigger, better, and brighter Canada.[8]

Despite the incident, Charles Peyton Jones, William H. Saunders, and W.H. Burke — pastors of the Campbell Chapel AME Church, Chatham Community

Church, and First Baptist Church respectively — jointly commended Leamington's mayor for "... allowing [them] to enjoy [their] liberties under the British flag."[9]

In another instance of racism during Emancipation Day, Mary MCleod Bethune, one of the speakers in Windsor in 1954 was denied a room at the Prince Edward Hotel because she was Black. However, the hotel gave a room to fellow speaker Eleanor Roosevelt. Consequently, the organizers, Walter Perry and Ted Powell, had to bring both of them to Detroit for accommodations.[10]

Growing awareness of the racism Blacks were facing led to Emancipation day festivities blending with elements of social and political protest. The occasion became a platform for organizers and speakers to advance democracy, equality, and social justice for African Canadians, rallying the nation toward social change.

WORDPLAY

Jim Crow Laws were laws that made the racist practices that restricted the public lives of African Americans legal. These laws limited or restricted where Blacks could and could not go and what they could and could not do because of their skin colour. This included eating in certain restaurants, swimming in public pools, and public transit seating.

CHAPTER TEN

THE LEGACY OF EMANCIPATION DAY: LESSONS FROM EMANCIPATION DAY

Oh, bread for the body there's got to be,
But a soul will die without liberty.
Pray for the day when the struggle is past,
Freedom for all! Free at last!
Freedom for all! Free at last!
— "No Easy Walk to Freedom,"
Peter, Paul, and Mary, *No Easy Walk to Freedom*, 1986.

What can be learned by looking at the 177-year history of Emancipation Day? Why is it important to us today? What do contemporary African Canadians have to say about Emancipation Day's legacy?

Emancipation Day commemorations were an interweaving of faith, thanksgiving, education, family, remembrance, protest, and community. Understanding this freedom festival provides insight into the early human rights movement in Canada and how African Canadians celebrated freedom since the end of slavery. It helps define the long-standing Black community in Canada, which is one of the four earliest groups that contributed to the building of the nation. We gain knowledge of the resilience, resistance, and determination put forward by African Canadians to break the shackles of slavery and to obtain equality as Canadian citizens. We get to learn about the dynamic composition of early Black communities and the diversity of early Black settlers. Through exploring August First celebrations, the tremendous contributions and sacrifices of African Canadians is uncovered.

Emancipation Day is an important site of memory, a place where people create reminders of the past. Remembrance is considered to be a form of resistance for people of African descent. By memorializing the experiences and courage of ancestors, through stories, songs, and other ceremonies, the silence of the past is broken. Countless stories are shared, heard, and passed on. Their memory lives on without end. Drawing on these memories provides strength to overcome present obstacles and offers inspiration to plot a course for the future. For young African Canadians, remembering their ancestors contributes to a sense of self and belonging, which is very empowering. It ensures that youth are aware of history and the important part they must play in fighting for social responsibility and equality. Further, we learn about the importance of education in breaking down barriers and building up the Black community. Blaine Courtney, current chair of the Owen Sound Emancipation Festival Committee and a descendant of early Black settlers, remarked:

> The one thing that has been obvious to me is the need to preserve and to share the stories and artifacts from out past. The better we perform this task the easier it will be for our youth to stay in touch with their roots. We also owe it to our entire community, White and Black, to ensure that as little as possible is lost and every chance to educate everyone about our history is taken.[1]

The first of August had a very powerful, unifying effect. It brought Blacks together in solidarity and joined Blacks and Whites to challenge injustice, mistreatment, and prejudice. The event also fostered community building among African Canadians, who were sometimes separated by the vast land and space of Ontario and the country. It united people of African ancestry and like-minded rights activists across the North American continent in establishing important networks with others who understood the strength in numbers.

Examining the history of Emancipation Day provides insight into the social transformation of African-Canadian culture, Canadian society, and the evolution of Emancipation Day itself. The improved social conditions for Black Canadians, especially compared to when they first arrived, shows the power of continuous protest. Some noticeable changes are integrated public schools, less discriminatory hiring practices, and the acknowledgement of the equal rights of people from different racial, ethnic, and religious backgrounds. The enactment of provincial and federal laws to enforce rights, including the Fair Employment Practices Act of 1951, the Fair Accommodations Practices Act of 1954, and the Canadian Charter of Rights and Freedoms of 1982, demonstrate progress. Because of these pieces of legislation, students can attend the school closest to them, regardless of their race. It is illegal for someone to be denied a job or a promotion or to receive less pay for equal work because of their race, gender, or place of origin. Businesses are breaking the law if they refuse to provide service to a person based on their race, religion, or gender. Fundamental human rights and freedoms are protected. As Canadians we can live and work anywhere in Canada, practise the religion of our choice, freely express our opinions, and vote for whomever we choose.

Emancipation Day has developed into a time-honoured Canadian tradition, celebrated in grand style. From the onset, Emancipation Day was a mix of pleasure and protest. Thousands of people have witnessed and taken part in the evolution of the commemoration. In 1967 the celebration's roots influenced Caribana, another popular African-Canadian tradition. One consistent characteristic is August First's reflection of a vision and hope of a better Canada. Dennis Scott of Burlington, Ontario, a descendant of early Black settlers, says, "Personally, the most exhilarating aspect of this transition in Emancipation Day celebrations was in the education of participants in local and Canadian Black history and culture."[2]

Freedom had to be fought for by slaves, abolitionists, Black soldiers, and civil rights activists so that African Canadians could exercise their full rights. The action plans were set, and the victories that followed were celebrated on Emancipation Day.

CHAPTER ELEVEN

FREEDOM TODAY

Cry freedom, cry deep inside where we are all confined.
— "Cry Freedom," Dave Matthews Band, *Crash*, 1996.

Young people today have a different understanding of freedom. Youth are generally more concerned about their personal freedom, such as strolling through the mall, going to the movies, and being able to buy the latest gadget. They are removed by many generations from the eras of African enslavement and the Civil Rights Movement. Because young people in Canada are considered equal under law and enjoy many freedoms, including access to education, health care, going where they want, as well as the freedom of expression, freedom of religion, freedom of peaceful assembly, and the freedom of association, you might ask, "What is there to fight for in Canada?"

Issues of inequality affecting young people in Canada continue to exist, and some have recently arisen. This requires their attention in order to effect change. Youth of the twenty-first century are confronted with materialism — the idea that success is driven by the attainment of possessions instead of the improvement of humanity. Another challenge faced by adolescents is the development of critical thinking — thinking for oneself and not blindly following others — in a society that seems to, at least on the surface, reward the opposite.

In many communities across Canada, youth are affected by a range of problems, including violence, bullying, gangs, drug abuse, isolation, poverty, racism, and lack of access to education. It can be said for urban, rural, and suburban neighbourhoods, on Native reserves, and in all provinces and territories. On the global scale, issues of poverty, exploitation, wars and conflicts, as well as mistreatment based on gender, race, and religion exist in the absence of human rights. In recent times, there has been a bellowing call for freedom and democracy by youth in places around the world, such as countries in the Middle East, North Africa, West Africa, and Europe.

Unfortunately, status as a Canadian citizen does not guarantee equality. Not all groups have an equal voice. Some voices, like those of African Canadians and First Nations, remain systemically silenced. Huge inequalities between the quality of life for Aboriginals and the general population persist. The obstacles of marginalized groups are not always examined with any kind of priority by governments at various levels. Although many Canadians have achieved a higher level of equality since civil rights movements and the abolition of slavery, social and economic inequalities continue to exist across races, genders, and abilities.

On a more positive note, there are youth in Canada and the world over of all races and cultures seeking to define freedom and equality for themselves. To make informed decisions, youth must examine local, national, and global issues. You are less likely to be held mentally captive by ideals that oppress you when you are able to think for yourself. Education on social issues encourages youth to become engaged in self-improvement and community-building activities. Further, knowledge empowers young people to advocate for issues of special interest to them, including the environment, child poverty, racism, homophobia, girls attending school in other countries, and access to food and fresh water. Understanding the roots of pressing issues is the best way to figuring out how to deal with them, and this requires looking to the past.

It should be clear that the struggle for equality continues, and similarly clear that youth are not too young to have a meaningful impact. It is up to youth to carry the movement for equal rights forward. Parents, educators, and other adults of influence have an obligation to pass on the torch by arming young people with essential historical information, equipping them with effective strategies, and providing mentorship. A link with the past can help to develop a healthy self image, give meaning to the present, and inspire youth to challenge injustice and discrimination with the outcome of a new wave of social change. Examining the rich history of Emancipation Day helps to foster new ideas of democracy and social justice. Participation in modern-day freedom festivals creates a bridge to the past while maintaining the significance of the commemoration in the present. True to its beginnings, the restoration of Emancipation Day, the triumphant celebration of a freedom movement, mirrors increasing efforts to free ourselves from mental enslavement, materialism, commercialism, and violence today.

As heirs of the future, younger generations are continuing the work for universal freedom. Young people are rightfully demanding that they be included in decision-making, so that they will be able to look forward to a world of promise, opportunity, and the right to exercise their full potential.

CHAPTER TWELVE

PICKING UP THE MANTLE

Let the freedom of youth captivate you.
— "Let the Song Last Forever," Dan Hill, *Frozen in the Night*, 1978.

There has been a revival of interest in Emancipation Day in many parts of Canada. Canadians are educating themselves about the African-Canadian experience, and there are scores of people in search of a more inclusive Canadian story, one that takes account of the contributions of various groups. Emancipation Day is a great learning opportunity for everyone. It is a way to understand and define freedom.

Adolescents are participating in Emancipation Day commemorations in growing numbers at revitalized events in Owen Sound, Windsor, Oakville, and Dresden. Organizers use a mix of old and new features to attract fresh crowds — multicultural attractions include speeches, parades, the Miss Emancipation pageant, sports tournaments, talent shows, history tours, displays, deejays, parties, midways, and lots of food from around the world.

African Canadians and youth should reclaim Emancipation Day because of its significance in history and benefits as an instrument of education, unity, and change. Likewise, it is necessary to understand that Caribana festivals evolved from Emancipation Day celebrations. The legacy and memory of African-Canadian pioneers and activists should be passed on by retelling stories of courage, sacrifice, and commitment.

The United Nations General Assembly has designated the year 2011 as the International Year for the People of African Descent. It offers an opportunity to become educated about the experience of Blacks in our nation and throughout the Diaspora. That includes discussion of the diverse experiences and contributions of enslaved African Canadians. At the core of August First celebrations is the concept of freedom as a human right, which resonates with people all over the world who have struggled to achieve freedom or who are still struggling to realize that dream. African-Canadians were vigilant in pursuit of their rights: the agitation for freedom by enslaved Africans throughout the New World, the fight for complete and equal freedom during the civil rights era, and the ever-changing meaning of freedom to African Canadians in the nineteenth and twentieth centuries.

Canadian youth are obliged to pick up where past generations left off in the fight for human rights in Canada. There is still much more to do around the issues of discrimination, systemic racism, and equality in our country. Fortunately, in a positive direction, numerous young Canadians of all races and backgrounds have been building on the efforts of early human rights advocates. They are activists who are passionate about equal rights and are working to improve the living conditions of groups that experience discrimination. Youth are educating themselves and others, courageously asking tough questions and taking grassroots action. There are a variety of youth-led initiatives that combat issues affecting freedom.

Social problems such as youth violence, rising high school dropout rates, and high unemployment rates for Black males are prevalent not only in Canada, but in other regions of the Atlantic World. African-Canadian Nkem Anizor has been very vocal and hands-on in dealing with issues that have a negative impact on the lives of Black youths in the Kingston-Galloway area of Scarborough just east of Toronto. The Neighbourhood Basketball Association was established by Nkem and fellow community activists, who have developed programs to assist and educate youth through mentorship, cultural education, recreation, and the fostering of business management skills. Nkem and her colleagues are committed to working with Black youth to improve their self-determination.[1] The Native Youth Sexual Health Network, founded in 2006 by Jessica Yee, who is of Native Canadian and Chinese descent, offers services and programs in Canada and the United States relating to sexual health for First Nations youth.[2]

While in grade eight, Shannen Koostachin and her friends spoke out against the federal government's failure to rebuild an elementary school. Children on the Attawapiskat First Nations reserve on James Bay in Ontario had been without a school building since the year 2000 and had been attending classes in portables that sat on contaminated land. Shannen advocated for the right of Native children to have a decent education, even going to Ottawa to confront the federal minister of Indian Affairs and Northern Development on the steps of Parliament Hill about the matter when she was thirteen. In 2009 the federal government decided to honour its commitment to build a school. A new school is scheduled to open in 2012.[3]

Free the Children was started by Craig Kielburger in 1995 when he was just twelve years old. He and eleven friends in Thornhill, Ontario, were motivated to action when they saw a horrific story about South-Asian child labour in the newspaper. The organization expanded to help children around the world overcome exploitation, poverty, as well as gain access to housing, food, and fresh water.[4] Toronto-based For Youth Initiative campaigns and provides innovative solutions to issues that create barriers to inner city youth. Their programs deal with youth and police, youth voting, newcomer youth settlement, and female youth to name a few. For Youth Initiative aims "to encourage

WORDPLAY

The Diaspora describes the migration or the movement of peoples of African descent around the world to places such as America, the Caribbean, Europe, and Canada as a result of the Transatlantic Slave Trade.

civic engagement and increase access to educational, recreational, economical, and cultural opportunities."[5]

One more example is the arts-based 411 Initiative for Change, which encourages young people to get involved in their communities and work with other young people to address global issues. The programs utilize music and art to battle prejudice and stereotypes, foster positive youth interaction, and bring attention to international charity causes. In support of national artistic talent, at least fifty percent of the content of their presentations is Canadian. All of these grassroots organizations mobilize and inspire young people to engage in acts of service to make a positive change in the lives of others.

Addressing pressing contemporary issues will require a large network of individuals and organizations. Coalition-building between community and labour organizations, women's groups, faith-based groups, and human rights groups is important in increasing public awareness and creating lasting change. Modern-day rights activists should consider using old, tried-and-true strategies such as organization and agitation coupled with new approaches like using social media — Facebook, YouTube, and Twitter.

Freedom was very much part of the national policy of Canada even before the dominion was formed, and so it continues to be. Freedom was placed on the political agenda by the disadvantaged and oppressed. We see that liberation struggles, as they relate to Blacks in Canada and other discriminated groups, have been a constant issue because rights are never simply given or granted. They have only been secured through vigilant campaigning. Even though the idea exists that basic civil rights and fundamental freedoms are protected and enforced by numerous pieces of legislation, today segments of our society are still not able to exercise their complete civil rights.

Freedom is fundamental to democracy, but wherever there is a democratic country, including Canada, there will be struggles for human and civil rights because democracy is an evolving process. A democracy changes and adapts as new challenges arise. The positive outcome hoped for is that changes will result in the further promotion of democratic values and benefits for the people, such as increased participation in society for everyone.

In the twenty-first century, there are many challenges to democracy all over the world. Poverty, sexism, racism, and other social injustices are just a few. Another challenge is suitable representation for all citizens, meaning, "are the politicians elected to represent us serving our best interests?" Globalization can also have a negative impact on democracy. When countries increase their economic relationships through the exchange of goods, services, and capital, inequalities can be created that affects democracy in the countries involved. When individual interests take priority over those of the group, people focus only on their own goals and fail to work together to better society. The push for international democracy poses another challenge: when certain countries, usually those with more power and wealth, become involved in telling other countries how to run their government, conflict inevitably arises.

There are several ways to ensure the advancement of Canadian democracy. For one, all citizens should participate in open discussions about democracy, even when they disagree. Secondly, citizens should engage in the democratic process, with the aim of influencing public institutions and modifying government and social practices so that they meet the needs of all Canadians and adequately reflect their shared values. The walls of oppression must be broken, so that one day, future generations will be able to celebrate true freedom.

NOTES

CHAPTER 1

1. *Public General Act, 3&4 William IV, c.73, Abolition of Slavery Act, Parliament Archives, United Kingdom*. The act is accessible online at *www.pdavis.nl/Legis_07.htm*.

CHAPTER 2

1. *An Act for the Abolition of Slavery throughout the British Colonies; for promoting the Industry of manumitted Slaves; and for compensating the Persons hitherto entitled to the Services of such Slaves*, Public General Act, Citation 3 & 4 Will IV, c.73. This legislation received the official short name of the *Slavery Abolition Act* in 1896.
2. LaBrew, Arthur R., *300th Year Celebration*, 256.

CHAPTER 3

1. *St. Catharines Journal*, October 15, 1835.
2. African Canadians were not welcome in all public establishments. Some businesses refused to serve Blacks because of their race.

3.   *Chatham Daily Planet*, August 2, 1899.

4.   The Nazrey Institute was changed to Wilberforce Educational Institute in 1873.

5.   Daniel was not a legally qualified doctor, but this was common for all doctors in the mid-1800s until medicine became a governed profession. He died in June 1894 and was honoured at that year's Emancipation Day observance.

CHAPTER 4

1.   Hamilton, James Clelland. "Slavery in Canada." *Transactions*. Volume 1, (1889–1890), 105.

2.   *Ibid.*, 106.; Riddell, William Renwick. "The Slave in Canada." *Journal of Negro History*. Volume 5, July 1920, 332.

3.   *Ibid.*

4.   McKnight, Alanna. "John Lindsay Report." *Breaking the Chains: Presenting a New Narrative of Canada's Role in the Underground Railroad; St. Catharines Journal*, November 12, 1835.

5.   Shadd, Adrienne, Afua Cooper, and Karolyn Smardz Frost. *The Underground Railroad: Next Stop, Toronto!*, (Toronto: Natural Heritage Books, 2005), 73.

6.   Hill, Daniel. *Freedom Seekers: Blacks in Early Canada*, (Book Society of Canada, 1981), 183.

7.   James Llewellyn Dunn sued the Windsor Board of Education in 1883 because his daughter Jane Ann was barred from attending the local public school because of her race. The court ruled in favour of the school board. He was elected as a school trustee for four terms.

8.   In recognition of their achievements, the city council of Windsor declared February 21 to 27, 2010, "James and Robert Dunn Week."

9.   *Hamilton Spectator*, August 2, 1888.

CHAPTER 5

1. *Provincial Freeman*, July 29, 1854.
2. Gordon, Robert. *A Sermon on the Morning of the 1st of August*, 1859, 5.
3. *Ibid.*, 10.
4. *Ibid.*, 23.
5. *Minutes of the Fifteenth Annual Conference of the AME for the Canada District*, July 16, 1853, 10.
6. Peter C. Ripley and others, eds., *The Black Abolitionist Papers, Volume II: Canada 1830-1865* (Chapel Hill: University of North Carolina Press, 1986), 77.
7. The conflict between the North and the South ended with the South surrendering and all enslaved African Americans being freed.

CHAPTER 6

1. Adrienne Shadd, email to author, January 2011.
2. Beth Allen, email to author, October 2010.
3. *Dresden Times*, August 6, 1891.
4. *Hamilton Spectator*, August 3, 1857.
5. *Toronto World*, August 2, 1884.
6. *Chatham Weekly Planet*, August 3, 1871.
7. As of May 2011, the official name of Caribana has been changed to the Scotiabank Caribbean Carnival Toronto after the Caribana Arts Group (formerly the Caribbean Cultural Committee), who are the owners of the trademarked festival Caribana, won a court decision to keep the name because it belonged to them. The CAG lost control of Caribana in 2006 and management of the festival was transferred to the festival management committee.
8. *Hamilton Spectator*, August 2, 1859.
9. *Ingersoll Chronicle*, August 21, 1907.
10. *Brantford Expositor*, February 10, 2007.
11. *Brantford Weekly Expositor*, August 5, 1859.

CHAPTER 7

1. Dorothy Turcotte. *Greetings from Grimsby Park: the Chautauqua of Canada* (Grimsby Historical Society, 1985), 40.
2. Nerene Virgin, email to author, June 2011; *Toronto Star*, July 27, 1964.
3. Nerene Virgin, email to author, June 2011.
4. *Chatham Daily Planet*, August 2, 1905.
5. *Owen Sound Sun Times*, August 4, 1905.
6. *Owen Sound Sun Times*, August 3, 1899.
7. *Dresden Times*, August 8, 1889.
8. Joanna McEwan. *The Story of Oro* (Oro: Township of Oro, 1987).
9. *Owen Sound Times*, August 3, 1899.
10. *Western Herald*, August 11, 1842.

CHAPTER 8

1. Mechanic's institutes were the predecessors of the public library.
2. *Windsor Daily Star*, July 25, 1952.
3. "Notes of a Speech Delivered at Chatham August 2, 1858," Fred Landon Papers, box 4220, William King File, University of Western Ontario Archives.
4. *Black Then: Blacks and Montreal 1780s–1880s* (Montreal: McGill-Queen's University Press, 2004), 199.
5. *Emancipator*, August 11, 1847.
6. *St. Catharines Standard*, August 5, 1938.
7. *Windsor Star*, August 7, 1956.
8. *Breaking Loose: A History of African-Canadian Dance in Southwestern Ontario 1900-1955*, 118, 119.
9. *Windsor Star*, August 3, 1954.
10. *Windsor Star*, August 4, 1954.
11. Isaac Holden was the captain of the Victoria Company No. 3, Chatham's all-Black fire brigade that formed in 1857, and the first African-Canadian city councillor in Chatham. Isaac Holden was the brother of Robert L. Holden.

12. *Toronto World*, August 2, 1882.

13. *Chatham Daily News*, August 8, 2006.

14. *Provincial Freeman*, August 5, 1854.

15. *British Colonist*, August 4, 1855.

16. *London Free Press*, August 4, 1896.

17. The Fourteenth Amendment was designed to guarantee full citizenship for Blacks and was intended to protect the legal rights of freed slaves and their descendants. It was passed by Congress in June of 1866 and was adopted by the states on July 9, 1868. The Fifteenth Amendment protected African-American men's right to vote. The legal bill was ratified on February 3, 1870. The 1964 Civil Rights Act made discrimination on the basis of race and gender in public places such as schools and workplaces illegal. Finally, the Voting Rights Act, signed by President Lyndon Johnson, outlawed the discriminatory voting practices in many southern states after the Civil War, such as requiring African Americans to take and pass a literacy test before being allowed to vote.

CHAPTER 9

1. Women of any race could not vote in Ontario provincial elections until 1917 and in Federal elections in 1920.

2. The children of Daniel G. Hill and Donna Hill are prominent in the arts world today. Their second son, Lawrence Hill, is a world-renowned author on the African-Canadian experience. Their first son, Dan Hill, is a well-known song writer and musician, and their daughter, Karen Hill, is a poet. For an overview of Daniel Hill's life, see the online exhibit, *The Freedom Seeker: the Life and Times of Daniel G. Hill*, on the Archives of Ontario website.

3. *Chatham Tri-Weekly Planet*, August 5, 1891.

4. *Toronto Star*, August 2, 1946.

5. *Chatham Daily News*, August 2, 2005.

6. *Leamington Post and News*, August 7, 1930; *Essex Free Press* August 8, 1930; Erica Bajer, "Not on the Books but True: Official Discrimination Hard to Nail Down in Chatham-Kent," *Chatham Daily News*, 2008.

7. Jim Crow Laws in the Southern United States required Blacks and Whites to be segregated in public places.

8. *Border Cities Star*, August 7, 1930.

9. *Ibid.*

10. Powell, Ted. *Interview with Lawrence Hill*. African Canadian Collection, Multicultural Historical Society of Ontario.

CHAPTER 10

1. Blaine Courtney, email to author, January 2011. Blaine's great grandfather, Abraham Courtney, was a fugitive slave from North Carolina. When he arrived in Owen Sound, Abraham worked as a farm hand.

2. Dennis Scott, email to author, April 2011. Dennis's great grandmother was originally from North Carolina.

CHAPTER 12

1. "Neighbourhood Basketball Association," *www.nbacanada.org/about.html*, accessed May 2011.

2. "Native Youth Sexual Health Network," *www.nativeyouthsexualhealth.com/aboutourfounder.html*, accessed May 2011.

3. Sadly, Shannen died in a car accident in May 2010 at the age of fifteen. Before June 2011, First Nations peoples could not have filed a human rights complaint because of discrimination under the application of the Indian Act by the federal government. They now have complete access to Canadian human rights law.

4. We Day was created by Free the Children in 2007 as an initiative aimed at educating and rallying Canadian public school children to raise funds and get involved in making a difference in the lives of other young people.

5. "For Youth Initiative," *http://foryouth.ca*, accessed on February 16, 2011.

SELECTED BIBLIOGRAPHY

BOOKS

Chamberlin, Agnes Dunbar. "The Colored People of Toronto," *Annual Report of the Women's Canadian Historical Society of Toronto*, 1897–1898.

Cooper, John. *Rapid Ray: the Story of Ray Lewis*. Toronto, Ontario: Tundra Books, 2002.

Gordon, Robert. *A Sermon on the Morning of the 1st of August 1859, by a Black Clergyman, the Reverend Robert Gordon, in St. Paul's Cathedral. London, Canada West, on the Occasion of the Celebration of the Twenty-First Anniversary of West Indian Emancipation, by the Colored Citizens of London, and Several other Places*. London, Ontario: Colonial Church and School Society, Mission to the Fugitive Slaves in Canada, 1859.

Green, Garth L. and Philip W. Scher, eds. *Trinidad Carnival: the Cultural Politics of a Transnational Festival*. Bloomington, Indiana: Indiana University Press, 2007.

Henry, Natasha. *Emancipation Day: Celebrating Freedom in Canada*. Toronto, Ontario: Dundurn Press, 2010.

Hamilton, James Cleland. *Osgoode Hall: Reminiscences of the Bench and Bar*. Toronto, Ontario: Carswell Co., 1904.

LaBrew, Arthur R. *300th Year Celebration: The Black Community: Music and the Fine and Secular Arts: The Detroit History that Nobody Knew (or Bothered to Remember) 1800–1900*. Detroit, Michigan: City of Detroit, 2001.

Robinson, Gwen and John Robinson. *Seek the Truth: A Story of Chatham's Black Community*. Chatham, Ontario: privately published, 1989.

Shadd, Adrienne, Afua Cooper, and Karolyn Smardz Frost. *The Underground Railroad: Next Stop, Toronto!* Toronto, Ontario: Natural Heritage, 2005.

Shadd, Ruth Ann. *Breaking Loose: A History of African-Canadian Dance in Southwestern Ontario 1900–1955*. Windsor, Ontario: Preney Print & Litho Inc., 1995.

Turcotte, Dorothy. *Greetings from Grimsby Park, the Chautauqua of Canada*. Grimsby, Ontario: 1985.

Wiggins, William H. *O Freedom!: Afro American Emancipation Celebrations*. Knoxville, Tennessee: University of Tennessee Press, 1987.

ARTICLES

Davis, Irene Moore. "Recognizing Windsor's First Councillors of African Descent," *Talking Drum Newsletter*, North American Black Historical Society, Volume 12, No. 13, March 2010.

Smardz Frost, Karolyn. "Communities of Resistance: African Canadians and African Americans in Antebellum Toronto," *Ontario History*, Ontario Historical Society, Volume 99, No.1 (Spring 2007): 44–63.

COLLECTIONS

The E. Andrea Shreve Moore Collection, Essex County Black Historical Research Society.

WEBSITES

"The Freedom Seeker: The Life and Times of Daniel G. Hill," Archives of Ontario, *www.archives.gov.on.ca/english/on-line-exhibits/dan-hill/index.aspx.*

"Grimsby Park," Closed Canadian Parks, *http://cec.chebucto.org/ClosPark/Grimsby.html.*

INDEX

ABOUT THE AUTHOR

Natasha Henry is a teacher, an educational curriculum consultant, and a speaker specializing in the development of learning materials that focus on the African experience. Author of *Emancipation Day: Celebrating Freedom in Canada*, she is also the education specialist for Breaking the Chains: Presenting a New Narrative of Canada's Role in the Underground Railroad, a project of the Harriet Tubman Institute at York University. She lives in Mississauga, Ontario.

OF RELATED INTEREST

**THE UNDERGROUND
RAILROAD**
Next Stop, Toronto!
Adrienne Shadd, Afua Cooper,
and Karolyn Smodz Frost
978-1896219868
$14.95

The Underground Railroad: Next Stop, Toronto!, a richly illustrated book, examines the urban connection of the clandestine system of secret routes, safe houses and "conductors." Not only does it trace the story of the Underground Railroad itself and how people courageously made the trip north to Canada and freedom, but it also explores what happened to them after they arrived. And it does so using never-before-published information on the African-Canadian community of Toronto. Based entirely on new research carried out for the experiential theatre show "The Underground Railroad: Next Stop, Freedom!" at the Royal Ontario Museum, this volume offers new insights into the rich heritage of the Black people who made Toronto their home before the Civil War. It portrays life in the city during the nineteenth century in considerable detail.

TO STAND AND FIGHT TOGETHER
Richard Pierpoint and the Coloured Corps of Upper Canada
Steve Pitt
978-1550027310
$19.99

In 1812, a 67-year-old black United Empire Loyalist named Richard Pierpoint helped raise "a corps of Coloured Men to stand and fight together" against the Americans who were threatening to invade the tiny British colony of Upper Canada.

Pierpoint's unique fighting unit would not only see service throughout the War of 1812, it would also be the first colonial military unit reactiviated to quash the Rebellion of 1837. It would go on to serve as a police force, keeping the peace among the competing Irish immigrant gangs during the construction of the Welland Canal.

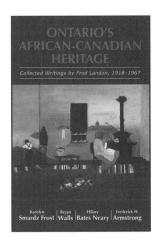

ONTARIO'S AFRICAN-CANADIAN HERITAGE

Collected Writings by Fred Landon, 1918–1967
Karolyn Smardz Frost, Bryan Walls, Hilary
Bates Neary, and Frederick H. Armstrong
978-1550028140
$28.99

Ontario's African-Canadian Heritage is composed of the collected works of Professor Fred Landon, who for more than 60 years wrote about African-Canadian history. The selected articles have, for the most part, never been surpassed by more recent research and offer a wealth of data on slavery, abolition, the Underground Railroad, and more, providing unique insights into the abundance of African-Canadian heritage in Ontario. Though much of Landon's research was published in the Ontario Historical Society's journal, Ontario History, some of the articles reproduced here appeared in such prestigious U.S. publications as the Journal of Negro History

Available at your favourite bookseller.

www.dundurn.com

What did you think of this book?
Visit www.dundurn.com for reviews, videos, updates, and more!

Marquis Book Printing Inc.

Québec, Canada

2011